FLY AWAY PETER

A Comedy in Three Acts

by

A. P. DEARSLEY

SAMUEL FRENCH LIMITED

LONDON

FOR AMATEUR PRODUCTION ENQUIRIES

UNITED KINGDOM AND WORLD EXCLUDING NORTH AMERICA

plays@samuelfrench.co.uk

020 7255 4302/01

Each title is subject to availability from Samuel French, depending upon country of performance.

FLY AWAY PETER

Produced at the St. James's Theatre, London, S.W.1., on August 12th, 1947, with the following cast of characters :

(In the order of their appearance)

TED HAPGOOD	*Aubrey Morris*
MYRA HAPGOOD	*Margaret Barton*
MRS. HAPGOOD	*Madoline Thomas*
ARTHUR HAPGOOD	*Michael Atkinson*
MR. HAPGOOD	*J. H. Roberts*
GEORGE HARRIS	*Peter Hammond*
PHYLLIS HAPGOOD	*Christine Russell*
JOHN NEILSON	*John Arnatt*
" DANDY " WESTMORE	*Maureen Hurley*

SYNOPSIS OF SCENES

The play is set in the living room of the Hapgood household in Streatham.

ACT I.

An evening early in March.

ACT II.

SCENE 1. A month later. 9 p.m. Saturday.
SCENE 2. The following evening.

ACT III.

SCENE 1. Two years later. An evening in late April.
SCENE 2. Two evenings later.

To face page 5—Fly Away Peter)

(Photo, Fobin Adler, F.R.S.A.

FLY AWAY PETER

ACT I.

Scene.—*The Living Room of the Hapgood household in Streatham.*

There is nothing peculiar about the Hapgoods and the living room reflects the tastes and habits of an ordinary Streatham family which is neither rich nor poor. The furniture has been there some time and was collected gradually. It is fairly solid stuff that has successfully managed to survive rough treatment at the hands of the children, though it shows its wounds. A heavy circular table, on a pedestal base, stands downstage, R. and a settee, downstage L. There is a sideboard against the R. wall and a boockase against the back wall to the L. of the door. A radiogram is in the upstage L. corner. A work basket, various chairs and a pouffe complete the main furniture. The door is in the back wall and leads to the hall. R. of the door is a large window of the push-up kind. This looks out on to a quiet street with a view of the houses opposite, though at present heavy curtains are drawn across it. The fireplace is in the L. wall. There is a clock on the mantelpiece. A lively fire is burning in the grate and adds to the already essentially cheerful atmosphere of the room.

When the Curtain *rises* Ted *is seen seated in the chair upstage of the table doing his homework. He is rising eighteen, wears a highly coloured school tie with blazer and flannels, and is now sailing through his French essay with perfect confidence. Enter* Myra. *She is sixteen, rather stockily built, and looks rather absurd in her short "gymmer". Her face is scarcely pretty and is marred at present with a black eye, though this does not detract from her obvious air of thoroughly enjoying life to the full. She comes down, carrying an exercise book, and sits at the table on* Ted's *left, chewing a thoughtful pen over her geometry problem. At length—*

Myra (*kneeling on the chair*).   Look, Ted.   From any point within a triangle perpendiculars are dropped—

Ted (*not looking up*).   Shut up.

Myra.   —on to the sides AB, BC, CA respectively.   Show that the sum of the squares on AP—

TED. *Will* you shut up.

MYRA. —BQ, CR is equal to the sum of the squares on—

TED } *(together).* { PUT A SOCK IN IT !
MYRA } { AR, CQ, BP.

TED. Do your own rotten homework.

MYRA. I can't.

TED. Then let me get on with mine.

MYRA. Give me a start. Go on—don't be a swab.

TED. No.

MYRA *(sniffing).* Oh well, I don't suppose you could do it if you tried. You ploughed matric. (TED *has bent over his work again and makes no reply.*) Lousy tick. (TED *looks up wrathfully and she goes on eagerly.*) I say, if I was to drop perps on to R— (*She rises to go round to him.*)

TED *(angrily).* Once and for all I'm not going to do your filthy geometry (*He waves her away.*)

MYRA. You are measly. You might just as well.

TED. How the hell d'you suppose you're going to pass matric if you get other people to do your brainwork ?

MYRA. Arthur used to help you.

TED. You cleverly remarked just now that I didn't get my matric.

MYRA. Ah, but you reached General Schools standard. That's quite good.

TED. Well then, get Arthur to help you.

MYRA. Fat chance of that. You know he never does.

TED. In that case there's only one thing for you to do—

MYRA. What's that ?

TED. As I told you before—put a sock in it.

(MYRA *purses her lips but says nothing. After a slight pause she rises and passes behind his chair, her fountain pen in her hand. Making a sudden dart she squirts ink over the work* TED *has done, then she runs across to the settee and sits.*)

You—you—*bitch* !

(*Enter* MRS. HAPGOOD, *bearing a tray with cutlery, etc. She is a woman of fifty, with steady eyes and features set normally in an expression of equal sweetness and severity. She pauses in the doorway.*)

MRS. HAPGOOD *(in a dangerous voice).* What was that, Ted ?

(TED *turns with a startled grunt.*)

(*She goes to the sideboard.*) What did you say ? (*She puts down the tray, etc.*)

TED (*mumbling*).   Well, she shouldn't have—(*He stops and hangs his head.*) Sorry, mother . . . .

MRS. HAPGOOD.   I should think so indeed. Now apologise to Myra.

(TED *turns to* MYRA *and struggles in vain for words.*   MYRA *sniggers.*)

Stop laughing, Myra.

MYRA.   Sorry, he looks so funny.

TED.   Oh hell—

MRS. HAPGOOD (*getting things ready on the sideboard*).   Now listen, Ted. This language may fit the Prefects' Room at school, but I won't have it in this house—do you understand ?

MYRA. Oh, mummy, you don't mind things like " damn." and " blast," do you ?

MRS. HAP. I do mind. Swearing isn't nice.

MYRA. Dad swears. (*She rises.*)

MRS. HAP. Oh no he doesn't.

MYRA. Oh yes he does. You should hear him on the golf course.

MRS. HAP (*flustered*). Now stop arguing. I don't like children to argue.

(*Exit* MYRA.)

TED (*piqued*).   And when do I cease to be a child ?

MRS. HAP.   All in good time.

TED.   Anybody would think I was a kid the way you talk.

MRS. HAP (*softly*). So you are . . . My kid . . . (*Being close to him she puts an arm round his shoulders.*)

TED (*shaking himself free*). Oh, for goodness sake, mother . . .

MRS. HAP (*taking the tablecloth from the sideboard, briskly*).   Now clear away your books. I want to lay the table. The others will be in in a minute . . . I can't think why you children don't do your homework in the other room—you could light the gas fire. (*Sweeping his books aside unceremoniously.*) Now come along. (*She opens the tablecloth and puts it on the table.*)

TED. Steady on, mind what you're doing.

MRS. HAP. Well, I didn't do that ! (*Pointing at the inky mess on his book.*) You'll be kept in for that—and serve you right.

TED (*with cold dignity*). You seem to overlook the fact that I'm in the Sixth Form and don't get " kept in " as you call it.

MRS. HAP. Don't you,.dear ? (*She goes back to the sideboard.*)

TED. Well, what do you think ! Do you seriously imagine any master would have the nerve to keep a prefect in ?

MRS. HAP (*only doing it to annoy*). I don't know. What is the difference between a prefect and an ordinary schoolboy ? (*She starts to lay the table.*)

TED (*with devastating sarcasm*). Oh, no difference, *of course.* A prefect can't give an ordinary schoolboy a hundred lines—oh, no ! He doesn't read the lessons at prayers—oh, no ! He doesn't have all the responsibility of keeping discipline at detention periods on Saturday mornings—of course not ! Third-formers do little jobs like that—naturally.

MRS. HAP. My goodness, what sarcasm ! (*She moves L. of* TED.)

(TED *swings on the back legs of his chair, scowling, hands in pockets.*)

TED. Well, you make me tired, mother. (*Then, seeing her smile, he lets himself down by laughing, in which she joins him delightedly.*) No, but honestly you do—.

MRS. HAP (*returning to the sideboard*). Do you think you never make me tired ?

TED (*rising and crossing to the settee*). Well, you make fun of me—just as though you thought it was a howling joke for me to grow older—.

(MYRA *enters and turns to the bookcase.*)

MYRA (*looking round and muttering*). Where is that perishing thing ?

MRS. HAP. What perishing thing ?

MYRA. My protractor. I thought you said swearing wasn't nice !

MRS. HAP. So I did.

MYRA. Perishing is a swear word.

MRS. HAP. Is it, dear ? (*She is above the table.*)

(MYRA *turns to go, but stops as a thought strikes her. She ·crosses to* MRS. HAPGOOD.)

MYRA. I wonder . . . Mummy, did you ever do geometry ?

MRS. HAP. I don't remember, dear, it's so long ago. I might recognise it if you showed me some.

MYRA. It doesn't sound very hopeful.

MRS. HAP. Oh, darling, do do something about that black eye as soon as you can. It's going to look dreadful tomorrow. Horrible game that hockey is.

MYRA. I've shoved a bit of steak on it. All it did was turn the steak blue.

Mrs. Hap (*sharply*). What steak was that ?

Myra. That lump that was on the kitchen table.

Mrs. Hap. You'd better not tell Dad and the others. I'm cooking
  it for their supper.

Myra. It'll taste all the richer.

Mrs. Hap. Don't be so horrible.

Ted (*chuckling*). Nothing like a black eye to make a steak nice and
  juicy.

Mrs. Hap. Ted . . . ! (*She crosses to the fire and moves the slippers to
  warm.*)

Ted. I'm going upstairs. (*He rises.*) Can't get any peace down
  here. (*He moves to the door.*)

(Athur *crosses* Ted *in the doorway and enters.*)

Hallo, you.

Arthur. Hallo.

(*Exit* Ted. Arthur *is dressed in City clothes. He is twenty-four, slim
  and well built. There is a moodiness about him which is reflected in
  the droop of his lips.* Mrs. Hapgood *goes swiftly to him and kisses
  him.*)

Arthur. Hallo, mother. (*He comes down C.*)

Mrs. Hap. Had a good day, dear ?

(*They meet down C.*)

Arthur. Oh, all right, thanks.

Mrs. Hap. Your hands are cold. (*It is an excuse to hold them.*) Is it
  freezing out ?

Arthur. It's a bit cold . . . Inclined to be foggy.

Mrs. Hap. I hope it won't make Dad and Phyl late.

Arthur (*vaguely*). What ? No—the trains are on time . . . (*He
  looks at her with sudden intentness, as though about to tell her something.*)

Mrs. Hap. What is it, dear ?

Arthur (*dropping his eyes*). Nothing . . . At least . . . I'll tell
  you later. I'll go and tidy up a bit. (*He turns to go and catches
  sight of* Myra's *black eye.*) My God, what a face !

Myra. Nark it.

Arthur. How did you do it ?

Myra. Hockey.

Arthur. Silly ass.

(*He goes out, leaving the door open.* MRS. HAPGOOD *crosses down* R. *below the table.*)

MYRA (*coming down to* MRS. HAPGOOD).   Here you are, mummy.

(MRS. HAPGOOD *takes the book and studies it with furrowed brow.*)

The other way up.   (*Putting it right way up for her.*)   Now then. That is any triangle ABC, and those are perps.—

MRS. HAP.   They're what ?

MYRA.   Perpendiculars, then—dropped on to the sides AB, BC, CA from the point O.   You have to prove that the sum of the squares on—

MRS. HAP (*decisively*).   No, I definitely never did geometry when I was at school.   (*Scornfully.*)   We used to draw jugs and flowers . . . daffodils . . .   I used to be very good at daffodils.   (*She hands* MYRA *back the book and goes to the sideboard for further supplies for the table.*)   Then we used to paint them in afterwards.   It was my favourite lesson . . .   (*Smiling reminiscently*).

(MYRA *gives a snort of deep contempt and takes the exercise book across to the settee.*)

MYRA.   *Daffodils* !   Didn't you ever do geometry in your life ?

MRS. HAP.   No, dear, I'm afraid not.   You see, in my schooldays teachers used to concentrate on making girls grow up—ladylike . .

MYRA.   But geometry isn't rude.   (*She flops on the the settee, her legs over the* R. *arm.*)   Anyway, who wants to be ladylike ?

MRS. HAP.   I want *you* to be.

MYRA.   Some hope !

MRS. HAP (*gently*).   At least my teachers taught me to sit in a chair gracefully.

MYRA.   Oh, I'm comfortable.

(*The key is heard turning in the front door.*)

There's Daddy—and the table not laid !   Is that you, Billy ?

MR. HAPGOOD (*off*).   Hallo, hallo!   (*He hangs his hat on the hall stand.*)

MRS. HAP.   Had a good day, dear ?   Did you get a seat on the train ?

(*Enter* MR. HAPGOOD.   *A mild-mannered man of middle age, humourously tolerant and kind.   He wears City clothes.*)

MR. HAP (*entering*).   I'm not quite sure, dear, but I think the kitchen is on fire.

MRS. HAP.   Damn—it's that steak . . .

(*She hurries out.*)

MYRA. Did you hear Mum swearing ?

MR. HAP (*catching sight of her black eye*). Oh, I say, look at you ! (*He stands by the R. end of the settee, looking at her.*)

MYRA. Oh, I know, I got it at hockey this afternoon.

MR. HAP. It's going to look ripe in the morning. (*He crosses to the mantelpiece.*) That damn' clock has stopped ! Perhaps I shouldn't have oiled it . . . (*He stands with his back to the fire.*)

MYRA. I suppose you want to sit here ?

MR. HAP (*apologetically*). Well, if it doesn't inconvenience you, Miss Hapgood.

MYRA. It's all right, I'll sit here. (*She moves to the pouffe.*)

(MR. HAPGOOD *gives her a playful slap with his paper as she passes.*)

MR. HAP (*sitting on the settee, R. end*). Wasn't it rather careless of you to get your eye in the way of the ball ? (*He reads his paper.*)

MYRA. It was that cad Brewster. She got rattled. She was supposed to mark me.

MR. HAP (*glancing over his paper*). She made a very good job of it !

MYRA (*grinning*). Oh, I got one back on her . . .

MR. HAP. What did you do, dear ?

MYRA. Just as she was going to shoot I kicked her in the pants !

MR. HAP. Seems to have been a nice friendly game.

(*Enter* MRS. HAPGOOD *with a cup of tea, loaf, bread-board and knife on a tray.*)

MRS. HAP. Cup of tea dear . . . Arthur says it's inclined to be foggy.

MR. HAP (*taking the tea*). Not as foggy as all that.

MRS. HAP. I hope it won't make Phyl late ? (*She takes the tray to the sideboard.*)

MR. HAP. I don't think so. The trains are on time.

(*There is a pause.*)

MYRA. This problem is impossible. I believe the wording is wrong. It must be.

(MRS. HAPGOOD *goes out.*)

MR. HAP (*eyeing her narrowly*). I shouldn't be surprised.

MYRA. I mean how can you possibly prove that—

MR. HAP (*hastily*). I don't know. (*He drinks his tea.*)

MYRA (*rising desperately*). Dad, have a go at it for me. You're jolly good at geometry. (*She sits beside him on the settee.*)

MR. HAP. My doctor said I was to keep away from geometry.

MYRA. Yes, I know that, but look. (*Showing the book to him.*) That's any triangle ABC. O is any point inside it. These are perps dropped on to the sides—

MR. HAP. What's this down in the corner ?

MYRA. Oh, that's Donald Duck. I always draw him when I'm worried.

MR. HAP. I thought it was your uncle George !

MYRA. Oh, come on, Dad. I do want this thing done.

MR. HAP. Take my cup. (*He hands it to her.*) What's the problem, then ? (*He takes the book and pencil.*)

MYRA. You've got to show that the sum of the squares on there, there and there is equal to the sum of the squares on there, there and there. (*Pointing at each " there."*)

MR. HAP. Oh, yes . . . (*He takes a look over his R. shoulder towards the exit. It is obvious he doesn't know how to begin.*)

MYRA. I think you ought to drop perps from R on to—

MR. HAP. No. No more perps. You've got enough. It already looks like Clapham Junction from the air now.

(ARTHUR *enters, an evening paper in his hand.*)

ARTHUR. Evening, Dad (*going to chair L. of table.*)

MR. HAP. Hallo. . . . Arthur, weren't you good at geometry ?

ARTHUR. No. (*He sits L. of table, opens out the paper and humps himself over it.*)

MR. HAP (*to* MYRA). Oh, aren't we a brainless lot !

MYRA (*bitterly*). I can see I shall end up by doing the darn thing myself.

MR. HAP (*studying the problem*). This is going to be very, very difficult.

MYRA. Go on, Dad, think *hard*. Something'll come in a minute.

MR. HAP (*sitting back*). That's all very well, but you know I'm not up to Matric standard. When I left Lower Middle B I began to feel the strain. I don't seem to have come on at all . . .

(ARTHUR *helps himself to water from the jug and reads his evening paper.*)

MYRA. Oh, I don't agree. You've done some quite good things since then.

MR. HAP. Have I, dear ? That's very nice of you . . . (*The solution occurring to him.*) Oh, this is perfectly simple. Let's cut these three squares out with a pair of scissors and paste them over the others. If they fit the whole thing is settled—

MYRA. Oh, don't be soppy, Dad ! That's not a proof.

ARTHUR (*irritably, looking up over his shoulder*). Let her go upstairs and think it out for herself.

MYRA. Quiet, dogsbody.

MR. HAP. You ought to really, you know.

MYRA. I can't. I've tried. Miss Rankin takes me for that and she'll be simply furious.

MR. HAP. Miss Rankin ? Is that the little fair, fluffy one who spoke to your mother and me on sports day ?

MYRA. Yes.

MR. HAP. She does geometry, does she ? . . . (*Grimly.*) Well, if she can do this I can.

(MRS. HAPGOOD *enters, carrying two plates of food, one of which she puts in* ARTHUR'S *place, the other in* MR. HAPGOOD'S.)

MRS. HAP. Come on, Billy, eat it while it's hot. Myra cut some bread for your father.

(MYRA *crosses to* R. *of* MR. HAPGOOD'S *chair.* MR. HAPGOOD *moves slowly across to his place, still concentrating on the problem.* MYRA *cuts a slice of bread and smacks it down on his plate.*)

MYRA. Carry on, Dad.

MR. HAP (*recklessly*). Let's try some of your perps. Where do you suggest we drop 'em ? (*He sits above the table.*)

MYRA. Start with this one—(*indicating*) R on to DE. I think it's got something.

MRS. HAP. Billy, get on with your food. It'll be stone cold in a minute.

(ARTHUR *starts his meal.*)

MR. HAP. All right, my dear. I'll just drop this perp. (*He does so.*)

(MRS. HAPGOOD *sits at the place* R. *of the table and pours out tea.*)

MYRA. Mustard ?

MR. HAP. Yes, please, dear.

(MYRA *helps him to mustard.* He is absorbed working on the problem.*)

MYRA. Pepper ?

MR. HAP (*without looking up*). Just a little, please.

(MYRA *energetically peppers his food.*)

(*Choking and spluttering.*) That's enough. Myra. I said a little, not a whole cloud of it.

MYRA (*laughing*). Sorry !

ARTHUR (*suddenly*). Are you going to be in tonight, Myra ?

MYRA (*surprised*). Yes. Why ?

ARTHUR. What about Ted ?

MYRA. How should I know ? Why, anyway ?

ARTHUR. I'll do that blasted problem if you'll promise to go right away for the evening.

(*They all look at him in surprise. The door bell rings.*)

Oh, lord—(*He rises quickly.*) Mother—I'm expecting a chap along tonight—

(*He breaks off and then goes out hurriedly.*)

MRS. HAP. What chap ?

MR. HAP. I don't know, I'm sure . . .

(*Voices are heard off. ARTHUR returns, looking relieved. He is followed in by GEORGE HARRIS.*)

ARTHUR (*sitting again*). It's only Pie-Face.

(*GEORGE HARRIS is an engagingly ugly youth of nineteen, with a face as honest as the day. He is thickset and slow and deliberate in his speech. He wears an overcoat and carries a bowler hat. His eyes at once fall on MYRA.*)

MR. HAP ⎫   ⎧Hallo, George.
MRS. HAP ⎬   (*together*).   ⎨Good evening, George, dear.
MYRA   ⎭   ⎩Wotcher, Pie-Face.

GEORGE (*coming C.*). Good evening, Mrs. Hapgood. Good evening, Mr. Hapgood . . . Hallo, Myra—(*catching sight of her black eye*) I say—good lord . . . !

MYRA. I know. I got it at hockey this afternoon.

MR. HAP. Is this the chap you're expecting, Arthur ?

(*They all laugh at this. GEORGE as well—though he doesn't know why.*)

ARTHUR. No, it's not !

GEORGE (*to MYRA*). I say, steak is a jolly good thing for a black eye.

MYRA. I've tried it.

MR. HAP (*pausing, with a forkful halfway to his mouth, sharply*). Steak ? What steak ?

MYRA. You're all right. Arthur's got the bit I used. He's eaten half of it.

ARTHUR (*with nausea*). You dirty little swine ! (*He looks at his plate with disgust.*)

MRS. HAP. Oh, get on with it, Arthur. I cut out the bit she used.

(*ARTHUR gives MYRA a look of cold distaste and continues to nibble half heartedly at his food.*)

GEORGE. I'm sorry to barge in while you're having your food, Mrs. Hapgood.

MRS. HAP. That's all right, George. Aren't you going to take your coat off ?

GEORGE. Well, I wasn't going to stay, thank you. I haven't been home from the office yet. I just thought I'd call round to see whether Ted or . . . (*a slight pause while he successfully manages not to look in* MYRA's *direction*) or anybody thought of going to the flicks tonight—

MYRA (*maliciously*). Who's " anybody " ? Mother ? (*She crosses to R. of George.*)

GEORGE (*grinning*). No, don't rot. (*He goes a little C.*)

MRS. HAP (*in mock disappointment*). Oh, George !

GEORGE (*horror-struck at his own faux pas*). I—I didn't mean I wouldn't take you, Mrs. Hapgood. Honestly, if you would like to go—

MRS. HAP (*gravely*). Thank, you, dear, I think that would be very nice —but perhaps I'd better not. I've got some sewing to do.

MYRA (*crossing below the settee to the L. end*). Besides, her husband might not like it.

GEORGE (*turning away*). Right-o . . . I'll go and ask Ted.

(MYRA *picks up the newspaper on the settee.*)

MRS. HAP. Unless, of course, Myra would do.

(GEORGE *turns back quickly.*)

MYRA (*reading the paper*). Dunno whether I will or not. (*To* ARTHUR.) Who is it that's coming to see you tonight ?

ARTHUR. Mind your own business.

MYRA. Yes, I know—but who ?

ARTHUR. I said mind your own damn business. Look here, Pie-Face, take her to the flicks for God's sake. When you get her there you can throttle her and shove her under the seat.

GEORGE. Oh, I'd love to—

MYRA. What !

GEORGE. Not throttle her, I don't mean—if she'll come . . .

MYRA. Are you going anyway ?

GEORGE. Yes.

MYRA. All right, call in on your way. I'll tell you whether I'm coming.

MRS. HAP. And if she decides to go, George, see that she's home by ten o'clock.

Myra. Oh lord, that means leaving in the middle of the big picture.

Mrs. Hap. Well, I suppose we could stretch a point. Make it ten-fifteen.

Myra. That's no good.

Mrs. Hap (*quietly*). You'll have to go and ask Ted, George.

(George, *with an appealing look at* Myra, *turns away to the door.*)

Myra. Pie-Face ! You dare !

(George *stops.*)

George ('*twixt devil and deep*). I—I don't care either way really.

Myra. Liar !

George. Well . . . (*another grin*).

Myra. Call in at quarter past seven or I'll bash your face in.

(Mr. Hapgood *chuckles.*)

Mrs. Hap (*sternly*). That will do. You shouldn't encourage her, Billy.

George. That's settled, then. I'll call for you at a quarter past seven. (*He moves towards the door.*)

Mr. Hap. Oh, George. Just a minute. Are you any good at geometry ?

George (*moving towards* Mr. Hapgood). Well, I didn't pass matric.

Mr. Hap. That doesn't surprise me in the least—(*handing* George *the book and pencil*) but have a shot at this. Myra, take it upstairs where it's quiet.

(George *moves to C.*)

Myra (*moving up to L. of* George, *reluctantly*). He can have a go at it, but he hasn't got much brain—have you, Pie-Face ?

George (*agreeably*). Not an awful lot.

Myra. Come on.

(*She leads the way to the door, snatching his hat away. She puts it on, jamming it down over her ears and doing a little dance to the door.* George, *in transports, turns to the others.*)

George (*at the door*). Isn't she a knock-out !

(*The door closes on them.*)

Mr. Hap. They have me in stitches, those two.

Arthur. Dad—about this chap that's coming—

Mr. Hap. Oh —yes, Well ? (*He has finished his meal and lights his pipe.*)

Arthur (*nervously*). His name is John Neilson. He's really coming to see you . . . and mother . . .

Mrs. Hap. Good gracious, what about ?

Arthur (*drawing a deep breath*). About that job I was talking about the other day.

Mrs. Hap. What job ?

Arthur (*between his teeth*). Don't you remember I was talking about a job that was going in Nigeria ?

Mrs. Hap. Arthur . . . ! You weren't serious about that ?

Arthur. I've practically got it.

(Mrs. Hapgood *looks at him aghast. Although she takes no part in the conversation that follows she is the emotional centre of the scene as she stares at* Arthur.)

Mr. Hap (*giving* Mrs. Hapgood *an uneasy look*). You'd better tell us all about it.

Arthur. This man Neilson has worked it for me—

Mr. Hap. I see . . . A bit sudden, isn't it ?

Arthur. You know perfectly well I've always wanted to go abroad.

Mr. Hap. Don't think I'm being obstructive, old boy—It's just the thought that you seem to have made up your mind without any reference to me—and your mother. I mean, we *are* interested.

Arthur (*bitterly*). What encouragement did mother ever give me to talk over a thing like that ? I've tried to do it several times and she's either laughed at me or frozen up . . .

Mr. Hap (*for something to say*). Of course, you've thought it over ? You're throwing up a good job—

Arthur. I know that. But I've got to do it. (*Tensely.*) I'm not going to spend the rest of my life in that damned office . . . living at home . . . a nice *protected* life.

Mr. Hap. You might want to get married some day.

Arthur (*sarcastically*). That would solve everything, of course. I could find a *nice* girl and live a *nice* quiet life—in Streatham ! Oh, I might move out of Streatham—into Balham, for instance. Balham is so different.

Mr. Hap. You want to make a radical change, is that it ?

Arthur (*more soberly*). Yes, Dad, I do. I want to *live*, not just exist. I want to—to start growing up; I haven't yet properly. I want to know what I'm capable of. Perhaps I'll be a failure—All right, but I want to know. *I've got to know.* What chance is there of becoming a real man if you spend all your life in a City office ?

Mr. Hap.   Are you asking me because I'm a City man myself ?

Arthur (*wretchedly*).   Dad, don't say things like that. You're different. It isn't fair to say things like that . . .

Mr. Hap.   Oh, I know it's not a glamorous life—although I think it has it's high spots. No, don't imagine I'm against your going. I only want you to get a balanced view of the proposition.

Arthur.   I've thought it all out, and I've *got* to go.

Mr. Hap.   Well, if you're quite sure, then, there's nothing more to be said about it. I can't help wondering, though, whether you've properly explored all the possibilities of your present way of living.

Arthur.   I haven't tried collecting stamps, if that's what you mean—

Mrs. Hap (*angrily*).   Arthur !

Mr. Hap (*patiently*).   No, neither have I. But I can get all the good music I want. I've read some good books—in between geometry problems !—played a bit of good club cricket—met some good sportsmen—

Arthur (*desperately*).   Dad, it isn't enough. None of that is a test for a man. It doesn't set him up against real life.

Mr. Hap.   Oh, well, it sounds as though you've made up your mind. (*He finishes the tea in his cup.*)

Arthur.   Yes, Dad, I have. (*In a snarling voice to his mother.*) I suppose you think I'm a swine because I want to leave you . . .

(Mrs. Hapgood *does not reply.*)

That's true, isn't it ?

Mrs. Hap.   It's no use me trying to say anything. You wouldn't understand . . .

Arthur.   I've got my own life to lead.

Mrs. Hap.   Yes, of course.

Arthur.   Why should I have to hang around at home ? Other fellows don't at my age.

Mrs. Hap.   I only want you to be happy, Arthur.

Arthur.   Yes, you say that—you pretend to agree with me—but you don't mean it.

Mr. Hap.   I think I'll have another cup of tea. (*He pushes his cup across.*)

(Mrs. Hapgood *pours out tea. The door bell rings.* Arthur *gives them an anxious look and goes out to open the door.*)

Arthur.   It's probably Phyl.

Mrs. Hap (*calling*).   That you, Phyl ?

Phyl (*off*). Yes, mother !

> (*She hangs up her coat on the hall stand.*)

Mrs. Hap (*calling*). In the oven dear—

Phyl (*from the hall*). All right—shan't be a minute.

> (*She goes off L. Arthur enters. He comes behind the settee.*)

Mr. Hap. Arthur, how long have you known this—John Neilson ?

Arthur. Three months. I met him in the City.

Mr. Hap. What is he like.

Arthur (*moving to the chair L. of the table*). Quite young. About thirty, I should say.

Mr. Hap. I suppose he's nothing to do with Neilson Swithin & Company, the shipping people ?

Arthur (*sitting*). Yes, he's old Neilson's son. The old boy is dead now.

Mr. Hap. Wait a minute. Isn't he rather a naughty boy ?

Arthur (*blankly*). Naughty boy ?

Mr. Hap. Wasn't there some sort of scandal over his divorce about a year ago ?

Arthur. Don't be so old-fashioned, Dad.

Mrs. Hap. I remember the case. He was married to a film actress— Pauline something-or-other. Isn't he a foreigner—a Dane— ?

Arthur. His father was Norwegian—his mother was English. He was born in Norway. What has all this got to do with his offering me a job, anyway ?

Mr. Hap. Nothing—but your mother and I like to know—

Arthur. Well, he's as rich as hell—and he's given me a chance I'll never have again in all my life. I couldn't turn it down, Dad.

Mr. Hap. And what exactly is he coming here for to-night ?

Arthur. I told you—to see you and mother.

Mr. Hap. That's very nice of him . . . I gather you mentioned that there might be some sort of trouble with your family ?

Arthur. Yes . . .

Mr. Hap. And he is coming here simply to put in a good word for you with me and your mother ?

Arthur. That's about it.

Mr. Hap. It seems a strange way for a millionaire to spend an evening !

Arthur. Oh, rot. How do you think he ought to spend his evenings ?

(Mrs. Hapgood *rises, comes to* Mr. Hapgood's R. *and moves plates to the sideboard.*)

Mr. Hap.   Supplying grounds for divorce, I should have said . . .

(Mrs. Hapgood *sits again.* Arthur *is about to make an angry retort when* Phyllis *enters carrying a plate containing her food. She is a dark, pretty girl of twenty-two, smartly but inexpensively dressed in a neat black frock. There is a suggestion of immaturity about her, but a brooding quality about her eyes makes you think there may be depths in her character not yet plumbed. She could have courage, fineness and sweetness. She puts her plate down in the place laid between* Mr. *and* Mrs. Hapgood.)

Phyl.   Hallo, everybody.   Am I wrong, or do I sense an " atmosphere " ?   (*She sits.*)

Mr. Hap.   Had a busy day, dear ?

Phyl.   Yes, Dad, I have.

Mr. Hap.   How were they all at the beauty parlour ?

Phyl.   Oh, all right.

Mr. Hap.   Did you give the Duchess her mud-pack ?

Phyl.   Yes, I did.

Mr. Hap.   Fancy being paid to throw mud at a Duchess !

Mrs. Hap.   Apparently Arthur has discovered a millionaire. . We have to entertain him tonight.

Phyl (*excited*).   Not Mr. Neilson ?

Arthur.   Yes.

Phyl.   Is he really a millionaire ?

Arthur.   Of course not, but I believe he's very wealthy.

Mrs. Hap.   What time is he coming ?

Arthur.   He didn't say.

Mrs. Hap.   That wasn't very considerate of him.

Arthur (*impatiently*).   He's coming straight on after a Board meeting. He didn't know what time it would end.   (*He rises.*)   Do you mind if I get down ?

Mrs. Hap.   No sweet ?

Arthur.   No, thanks.   (*He pushes his chair in and crosses to the settee where he sits at the* R. *end and lights a cigarette.*)

Phyl.   So at last I'm going to meet the fabulous Mr. Neilson ! Arthur, have you really got the job ?

(Mr. Hapgood *re-lights his pipe.*)

Arthur.   As good as.

MRS. HAP.   So you told Phyllis all about it ?

ARTHUR.   More or less—

MRS. HAP.   A family should share each others' secrets—

PHYL (*shortly*).   I don't know what you mean by " secrets," but Arthur and I are good pals and so—

MRS. HAP (*pleading*).   Well, aren't we all good pals ?   Do you think I wouldn't understand ?

PHYL.   You still treat us like children, mother.   I have to be in by eleven every night.

MRS. HAP.   Do you realise that when I was a young girl I wasn't allowed out after eight o'clock ?   *Eight* o'clock, mind you—

PHYL.   So you met Dad secretly.

MRS. HAP.   That was our romance—

ARTHUR.   Then let Phyl have *her* romance—that's only fair.

MRS. HAP (*startled*).   What romance ?   Phyllis ?

PHYL.   There isn't one (*to* ARTHUR) Fathead.

MRS. HAP.   I wouldn't mind if there was one, Phyl—providing you told Daddy and me about it.

PHYL.   Once and for all, mother, there isn't.   How on earth *can* I have a romance without a front door key ?   It isn't humanly possible.

(MR. HAPGOOD *finishes the tea in his cup.*)

MRS. HAP.   But why should you have a door key ?   This is your home.   You children come and go as you please.   You treat the place just like a hotel.   Anyway, I know I'm right.   It's tempting Providence for a young girl—

PHYL.   But *I'm a woman.*

MRS. HAP (*smiling indulgently*).   For a young woman, then—to be out late at night.   I'm older than you, dear, and I know.

PHYL.   But I'm old enough to look after myself.   (*To her father, desperately.*)   Don't you think so, Dad ?

MR. HAP (*steadily*).   Your mother knows what she's doing, Phyl.

(MYRA *enters, still wearing* GEORGE'S *hat.*   GEORGE *follows her in, on her L.*)

MYRA.   You'll have to have another crack at it, Dad.   Pie-Face doesn't seem to have caught up with his age—(*as* PHYLLIS *catches sight of her black eye.*)   Hockey.   Cad Brewster.   Rattled.   Full story on application to Dad.

MR. HAP.   Did you try dropping perps, George ?

MYRA.   Drop perps !   I had to go after him with a dustpan and brush.

(*To* George.) You'd better bung off. Be back by quarter past seven.

Mrs. Hap. You're going, then ?

Myra (*carelessly*). Probably. I haven't quite decided yet.

Mrs. Hap. It seems a shame to make poor George rush about just on the off chance.

Myra. Good for his liver. What are you waiting for, Pie-Face ? Go on—(*Shooing him away.*)

George. Could I have my hat ?

Myra (*giving him the hat*). Oh, here you are. Go along . . . (*Pushing him out of the room.*) Can't stand the sight of you tonight. . . .

(George *starts to go off* L. *through the hall.*)

Front door . . .

(George *turns and goes off* R. ; Myra *goes off* L.)

Arthur. Have we any whisky in the house ? (*As* Mrs. Hapgood *appears not to have heard.*) Mother—have we any whisky in the house ?

Mrs. Hap. What ? Yes, there's a bottle in here—(*She goes to the sideboard and gets a bottle from the cupboard. She begins collecting the used crockery.*)

Arthur (*rising*). Good. I'll light the gas fire in the drawing room. (*He crosses to the fire.*)

Mrs. Hap. The curtains are not up.

Arthur. Oh, lord—(*he stands with his back to the fire.*)

Phyl. Can't we put them up ?

Mrs. Hap. No, dear, Mrs. Bailey hasn't finished the spring cleaning yet.

Phyl (*rising*). Can't Arthur and I tidy up a bit ?

Mrs. Hap (*irritated*). Certainly not. Sit down and finish your meal, Phyllis. (Phyllis *sits.*) All this silly fuss just because that man is coming here . . . (*She picks up the tray of used crockery.*) If this room is good enough for us it's good enough for him. Have you finished, Billy ?

(Arthur *sits on the settee.*)

Mr. Hap. Yes. I don't think I'll have any pudding. I'll take that out—

Mrs. Hap. Thank you, dear.

(*She puts the tray on the table and goes out.*)

MR. HAP (*rising*). Would anybody care to assist with the washing up ? (*Silence.*) No—well, I hadn't much hope . . .

(*He picks up the tray and goes out.*)

PHYL. Arthur, what's he like ?

ARTHUR (*rising*). Nice chap.

PHYL. That's everything, of course.

ARTHUR (*moving L.C.*). Well, if you mean has he any sex-appeal—the answer is—you'd be surprised !

PHYL. Is he young ?

ARTHUR. Can't be more than thirty.

PHYL (*rising with her plate*). Oh ! I think I'll go and change . . . Mother was difficult, I suppose ?

(ARTHUR, *before answering, goes to door and closes it.*)

ARTHUR. Awful ! Look here, Phyllis, shall I tell you something ? (*He comes to the chair L. of the table.*)

PHYL. Yes.

ARTHUR (*standing behind the chair*). One of my reasons for taking this job is to get right away from her. She makes me feel as though— as though there's no air—

(PHYLLIS *takes a tray from under the sideboard and during the following clears the table on to it.*)

PHYL (*briefly*). I know. Mother's like an internal itch that you can't scratch—

ARTHUR. Does she do that to you as well ? (PHYL *nods.*) Doesn't it irritate you every time when she asks you the same damn fool questions ?—" What sort of a day have you had ? " " Did you get a seat on the train ? " . . . She doesn't ask casually as anybody else might ; she *probes* as though every little thing about you was vitally important for her to know. I get a feeling of triumph when I manage to hide something from her. Do you ever feel like that ?

(PHYLLIS *has put the tray on the chair above the table and the bread on the sideboard. She removes the tablecloth and folds it.*)

PHYL. No, I haven't reached that stage. Perhaps it's because I'm rude to her instead ; it's another way of letting off steam. Don't you think you're letting yourself get rather morbid about it ?

ARTHUR (*gloomily*). Probably. In fact I know I am.

PHYL (*putting the cloth on the tray*). Well, all I can say is it's a jolly good thing you are going away. It will give you a chance to get the whole thing in perspective. . . . What is he really like ?

ARTHUR.   He's half Scandinavian. . . .

PHYL.   That tells me a lot ! (*She pushes in the two chairs R. of the table.*)

ARTHUR.   Well, he's tall, good looking—he has good taste.

(PHYLLIS *puts the tray on the table. MYRA bustles in. She runs to R. of the window.*)

MYRA (*in great excitement*).   I say—there's a perfectly bee-yewtiful car just stopped outside ! It looks as though the man is coming here—

ARTHUR (*miserably*).   Oh, hell . . .

MYRA (*shouting through the door*).   Ted ! Come and look at the marvellous car ! (*She rushes to the window, parting the curtains to look out.*)

PHYL.   Come along, somebody—help me . . .

(*Enter* TED. *He joins* MYRA *at the window.* PHYLLIS *puts the flowers from the sideboard on the table.*)

TED.   What is it, d'you know ?

MYRA.   No, but have you ever seen such a beauty !

(*Enter* MRS. HAPGOOD.)

MRS. HAP (*moving R. above the table*).   What are you children making such a row about ?

MYRA.   He's come, Mummy—Arthur's friend !

MRS. HAP.   Come away from the window, you two.

(PHYLLIS *hastily picks up the tray. The door bell rings.*)

PHYL.   Let me get out with this lot first . . .

(*Enter* MR. HAPGOOD *with an apron tied round his waist.*)

MR. HAP (*coming behind the settee*).   One of you had better open the door. (*He hurriedly pulls off the apron and stuffs it under a cushion on the settee. He moves round to the fire and stands with his back to it.*)

ARTHUR.   Will you, Phyl ?

PHYL.   No fear !

(*She rushes out with her tray.*)

MYRA.   I will.

(*She dashes out.*)

ARTHUR   (*bawling*).   No—Myra—let me—Myra . . . (*But she has gone.*)   I'd like to take a strap to that little beast !

(MRS. HAPGOOD *gets her sewing from the work box down R. There is a*

*murmur of voices from the hall. TED is up R.C. between the window
and the table ; ARTHUR moves behind the settee; MRS. HAPGOOD sits in
the chair R. of the table. MYRA enters and stand L. of the door. JOHN
NEILSON enters and stands in the doorway. He is dark, with clever
eyes, easy manners and any amount of natural charm.)*

MYRA.   We're all in here.   Excuse the smell of onions . . .

ARTHUR.   Hallo, Mr. Neilson.   Jolly good of you to come—

JOHN.   Not at all.   *(He comes down C.)*

(MYRA closes the door.)

ARTHUR *(introducing)*.   My mother . . . Mother, this is Mr. Neilson.

MRS. HAP.   How do you do, Mr. Neilson ?

JOHN.   How do you do ?

ARTHUR.   My father—

MR. HAP *(moving C.)*.   I'm pleased to meet you.

JOHN.   I'm pleased to meet you, sir.

(They shake hands.)

ARTHUR.   My young brother, Ted—

JOHN *(turning to TED)*.   How are you, Ted ?

TED.   Fine.   I like your bus.

JOHN.   It's a nice car, isn't it ?

ARTHUR.   My sister—

MYRA *(coming down C., cutting in)*.   Myra.   How d'you do, Mr. Neilson?
Fine, thanks.   How d'you do, Miss Hapgood ?   Fine . . .   *(As
JOHN stares at her black eye.)*   I got my black eye at hockey.

JOHN *(with a sigh of relief)*.   Ah, good !

MYRA *(staring)*.   What did you say ?

JOHN.   The fact is I once sympathised with a man for having broken
his nose—and he said he hadn't !   So I was wondering if your
black eye was real.

MYRA.   It's real enough !   It was a hell of a conk !

ARTHUR.   Let me take your hat.

JOHN *(handing it over with his gloves)*.   Thank you.

ARTHUR.   Ted.   *(He passes the hat and gloves to TED.)*

*(TED goes out, puts them on the hall stand. ARTHUR crosses to R. above
the table.)*

MR. HAP.   Won't you sit down, Nr. Neilson ?

JOHN *(sitting on the settee, R. end)*.   Thank you.   *(After an awkward
pause.)*   It's cold tonight . . .

Mr. Hap. Oh, yes—seasonable—we've got a bit of a fire—not much.

Arthur. Would you like a drink ? (*He starts towards the sideboard.*)

John. Not just now, thank you.

Myra (*severely, to* Arthur). You should have asked him first if he'd like a wash.

Arthur (*in a savage undertone*). Shut up !

Mrs. Hap. Myra !

(Ted *enters, shuts the door and comes above the* R. *end of the settee.*)

John. No wash, thanks.

Myra (*coming in to the* R. *end of the settee.*) That's rather fortunate—because Phyl is in the bathroom !

John. Phyl— ?

Mr. Hap. Phyllis is my eldest daughter.

John. Oh—yes . . .

Arthur. She works in Poireau's, in Bond Street.

Myra. It's a beauty parlour. I may go there.

(Ted *and* Myra *giggle.*)

Arthur. She'll be down in a minute.

(*Under the concentrated scrutiny of* Myra *and* Ted, John *shifts a little in embarrassment.*)

John. You—er—find it healthy living in this part of the world ?

Ted. The common is fine in the summer.

John. Oh, you've got a common ?

Myra. Yes—grass, you know—wide open spaces—green belts—

Arthur. What about having these kids outside, Dad ?

Ted } (*together*). {Who's a kid ? (*He crosses to* Arthur.)
Myra }   {I'm staying right here ! (*She follows* Ted.)

Mrs. Hap. Don't be unkind, Arthur. This is the only warm room in the house this evening.

John. You know, this is fun ! I don't think I've ever seen an entire family at home before.

(Mrs. Hapgood *is seated by herself on the* R. *of the table, a lonely figure separated from the rest. She occupies herself with some sewing.*)

Mrs. Hap. And have you no family, Mr. Neilson ?

John. Unfortunately, not.

Mrs. Hap. No brothers or sisters ?

John. No, I was an only child. A spoilt one, I'm afraid !

Mrs. Hap. It looks as though we shan't be complete ourselves very much longer. Arthur tells me you want him to go out East.

Mr. Hap (*mildly*). The place is West Africa, my dear. That is hardly " out East."

Myra (*interested*). Go on ? (*To* Arthur.) You going abroad ?

Arthur. Shall we discuss it later, when the kids have gone ?

Ted. Where am I supposed to be going ?

Arthur. Can't you go the pictures with George and Myra ?

Ted. Use your intelligence, laddie.

Myra. Anyway, I haven't said I'm going yet.

Arthur. Mother, she ought to go. She told George—

Myra. I told him I *might* go.

Arthur. You can't let him down—

(*A squabble is beginning to blow up. Their voices rise.*)

Myra. Who's letting him down ? I'm training him—and it's nothing to do with you, anyway, silly ass—

Arthur. Silly ass yourself—

Ted. That's right, Myra—don't let him bully you . . .

(*They argue shrilly and unintelligibly until :*)

Mr. Hap (*clapping his hands*). Children, children ! (*As silence ensues he indicates* John. *To* John.) The family at home, Mr. Neilson. . . !

Mrs. Hap. But we aren't going to discuss anything secret, are we ? Anyway, it isn't often we have such an interesting visitor !

Ted (*crossing to the R. of the settee*). Are you a traveller, sir ?

John (*taking out a cigarette case*). Yes—a bit, I've been to one or two places—

Mr. Hap (*forestalling him with a packet of cigarettes*). Here, have one of these, Mr. Neilson ; don't smoke your own.

(Myra *sits above the table.*)

John (*accepting*). Oh—thank you.

Mr. Hap. Got a light, Ted ?

Ted. Yes, Dad. (*He takes a lighter from his pocket and lights* John's *cigarette.*)

Mr. Hap. Now, tell me, Mr. Neilson, what sort of place is this Nigeria ?

John. Oh, lots of ants and flies and things, you know !

Mrs. Hap. Sounds horrible.

JOHN. Oh, no, it's not as bad as all that. The climate is tropical, but it's quite agreeable when you get used to it.

MR. HAP. And the job—do you think it will suit my son ?

JOHN. Well, Mr. Hapgood, it's very different from the sort of work he's doing here—but that's what he's after, I understand.

MYRA. He won't go native, will he ?—with a ring through his nose.

JOHN. Not quite !

MRS. HAP. Darling, if you're going to the cinema you'd better go and get ready.

MYRA. I can't till I've done my geometry.

JOHN. Do you do geometry ?

MYRA. Yes. (*She crosses quickly to him thoughtfully.*) Yes . . . Do you ?

JOHN. Yes, I was rather good at it at school.

MYRA (*eagerly*). You couldn't have a go at an impossible problem, could you ?

MR. HAP. Now, Myra, Mr. Neilson hasn't come here to do your homework. ,

(MYRA *moves above the settee.*)

(*To* JOHN.) Tell me, Mr. Neilson—what sort of work would my son have to do ?

JOHN. Well, for the first three or four months he'll be travelling round and getting familiar with his surroundings—getting some knowledge of the commodities we deal in.

ARTHUR. It sounds wonderful.

MRS. HAP. And he'll get paid for that ?

JOHN. Why, yes—certainly.

TED. Couldn't I come and carry the commodities ?

(MYRA *and* TED *roar with laughter.*)

MRS. HAP. Will you two go upstairs ?

MYRA. Can't he do my geometry, mum ?

JOHN. May I, Mrs. Hapgood ?

MYRA. Certainly you may ! I'll go and fetch it.

(*She goes out, shutting the door.*)

MRS. HAP. Well, I thought you'd come here to talk about Arthur.

JOHN. We'll have a long chat later.

ARTHUR. Yes, when the room is a little less crowded—

(TED *moves up to the window.* PHYLLIS *enters. She has changed her frock, shoes and stockings, and has overhauled her hair and make-up. The result is delightful. She is a little nervous and excited.* JOHN *rise slowly.*)

ARTHUR (*up R.*).   Oh, this is Phyllis, Mr. Neilson—my other sister.

PHYL (*coming down to* JOHN).   How do you do ?

JOHN (*rising*).   How do you do, Miss Hapgood.   Arthur has told me about you.

(*Enter* MYRA. *She pushes between* PHYLLIS *and* JOHN *as they are shaking hands. She gives* JOHN *her exercise book.*)

MYRA (*eagerly*).   That's any triangle ABC—

(PHYLLIS *crosses down L. and sits on the pouffe.*)

—O is any point inside it.   You've got to show that the sum of the squares on there, there and there is equal to the sum of the squares on there, there and there.   Take my pencil.

JOHN (*studying the problem*).   H'm . . .   Let's go to the table . . .

ARTHUR.   If it bores you . . .

(JOHN *crosses to the chair L. of the table and sits. He waves* ARTHUR *into silence and draws a new diagram.* MYRA *kneels on the chair above the table.* ARTHUR *stands R. above the table.* TED *stands between* MYRA *and* JOHN.)

MRS. HAP.   Really, Billy, we can't have Mr. Neilson embarrassed like this.

MR. HAP (*crossing to* JOHN).   No, no, Mr. Neilson,   Don't you bother. It's a very simple little thing.   I'll do it for them later.   (*He coughs as the ironic glances of the family fall on him and then joins* TED, MYRA *and* ARTHUR.)

JOHN.   Let's join OA, OB and OC.   (*He does so.*)   That gives us three right-angled triangles—here, here and here.   Correct ?

MYRA.   Granted.

MR. HAP.   But what good does it do ?

JOHN.   It's our old friend Pythagoras.

MR. HAP.   Oh, yes.   " The square on the hypotenuse of a right-angle triangle is equal to the sum of the —."

(*There is a tap at the window.*)

MYRA.   Oh, be quiet, Dad.   That'll be Pie-Face at the window.   Let him in, Ted.

(TED *goes to the window and throws it open.* GEORGE *clambers through it into the room. He comes to R. of* MYRA.)

JOHN. Therefore OA squared equals OR squared plus AR squared—

MYRA. I'll let you have that as well. Sorry, Pie-Face, I can't come to the pictures. I've got to do my homework.

MRS. HAP. My scissors, Arthur—I think they're on the mantelpiece—

(ARTHUR *crosses behind the settee to the mantelpiece.* PHYLLIS *hands him the scissors from mantelpiece and he crosses below the settee to* MRS. HAPGOOD.)

JOHN. But OA squared also equals OP squared plus AP squared—

GEORGE. The one-and-ninepennies will be full . . .

MYRA. Shut up. Mr. Neilson, please go on.

(*In taking the scissors from* ARTHUR, MRS. HAPGOOD *holds his hand and looks at him pleadingly.*)

JOHN. So OR squared plus AR squared equals AP squared plus OP squared—

(ARTHUR'S *chin lifts in a sudden defiant movement and he withdraws his hand. Deliberately he turns away from* MRS. HAPGOOD *and joins the party behind* JOHN'S *chair. Her eyes follow him, hurt and unhappy.*)

In the same way OP squared plus BP squared equals OQ squared plus BQ squared—(*he is swiftly writing this down as he goes along*) and OQ squared plus QC squared equals OR squared plus RC squared . . .

(MRS. HAPGOOD *rises and, with head lowered, goes slowly from the room. The others, apart from* ARTHUR, *are too absorbed in the problem to notice.*)

Now let's have a look. . . . I've got three equations. Right, I'm going to add all the left-hand sides together and then all the right . . . (*Triumphantly.*) Ah, I thought so !—There's an OQ squared on both sides, so out they go—(*Striking them through.*) An OP squared and an OR squared . . . (*Striking them out also.*)

(*The group gathers closer. As* JOHN *concludes in a sing-song rhythm their heads come down together on the last three phrases.*)

Leaving AR squared plus PB squared plus QC squared equals AP squared plus BQ squared plus RC squared . . . (*He raises his head and looks at* PHYLLIS.)

(PHYLLIS *is at first a little startled. Then she gives him a friendly smile.* JOHN *crosses to her.*)

MYRA. Gosh ! That will put the kibosh on old Rankin !

TED. I say ! Can he do French ?

PHYLLIS (*to* JOHN). Successful ?

JOHN (*smiling*). I think so . . .

MYRA (*straightening up, exercise book in hand*). Now then, Dad, shall I take it through slowly for you ?

CURTAIN.

ACT II.

SCENE I.

SCENE : *The Same.   A month later, 9 p.m. Saturday.*

MYRA *is alone in the house. She is lying flat on her stomach by the fire, reading a book. Occasionally she dips into a bag of sweets by her side. The door bell rings. She rises reluctantly and goes to answer it, still reading the book which she throws down on the chair by the door as she goes out. She switches on the hall light and opens the front door.*

GEORGE (*off*).   Hallo.

MYRA.   Pie-Face, what on earth do you think you are doing ?

GEORGE (*off, but following her in and standing in the hall*).   I thought I'd come and . . . cheer you up.

MYRA (*bluntly*).   How ?

GEORGE.   I thought we might have some music.   I've brought some duets round.   (*He indicates a bundle of music he is carrying.*)

MYRA (*coming above the settee*).   I told you I couldn't see you tonight. In any case you can't come in—we've got no chaperone.

GEORGE (*blankly*).   Chaperone ?

MYRA (*firmly*).   Chaperone.

GEORGE (*in the doorway*).   What d'you want a chaperone for ?

MYRA.   Too protect me, of course.

GEORGE (*amazed*).   Who from ?

MYRA.   Dirty dogs like you !

GEORGE (*horrified*).   Good Lord ! I'd never . . .   You don't think I'd ever . . . ?   Why, I wouldn't—

MYRA (*briskly*).   Anyway, you can't come in.   There'd be a row if mother found out.   Silly, but there it is . . .

GEORGE (*resignedly*).   Oh, well, I'd better go—(*He turns away.*)

MYRA.   Wait a bit.   We can talk through the window.   They can't object to that.

GEORGE (*eagerly*).   That'll suit me fine.   (*He puts the music on the seat in the hall.*)

MYRA. Go on, then, Don't trample on our geranium.

(GEORGE *goes out.* MYRA *opens the window and* GEORGE'S *head, bowler-hatted, appears.*)

You can put your head inside if you like.

(GEORGE *does so and leans on the window sill.*)

GEORGE. Question is—do I take my hat off or not ? You see I don't know whether I'm in or out !

MYRA (*sitting on the window sill at R. of window*). If you take it off I shall have to hang it on the hallstand. That'd be daft !

(*They giggle at the thought.*)

GEORGE. Where is everybody ?

MYRA. Dad and mother have taken Arthur out to the theatre—sort of final celebration before he sails—and Ted's at school rehearsing for the Prefects' Concert. Phyl went out about two hours ago all dolled up, so I suppose it's one of the boy friends.

(GEORGE *climbs in and sits on the window sill* L. *of* MYRA *with his feet on the chest.*)

GEORGE. Bit tough you being all alone.

MYRA. Laddie, it's a pleasure. Comfortable ?

GEORGE. Fine.

MYRA. Ever since Arthur said he was going abroad there's been a deep depression over Iceland.

GEORGE. Your mother's fed up about it, isn't she ?

MYRA (*nodding*). M'm.

GEORGE (*pontifically*). The birds have to fly away from the nest some time—

MYRA. —Shakespeare ! (*She produces a bag of sweets.*) Have a sweet.

(GEORGE *takes one out and inspects it, then puts it back again. By his look and hands it's all pretty sticky.*)

GEORGE. No, thanks. I think I'll have a cigarette. (*He takes a packet from his pocket. He sees her watching him and offers it.*) Like one ?

MYRA (*carelessly*). Yes, I think I will. (*She take one.*) What are they—Virginian ?—because I like Turkish myself. Still, I'll have one! (*He lights it for her. She splutters*). I wonder what people smoke for ?

GEORGE. It soothes their nerves.

MYRA. Doesn't seem to make any difference to mine.

GEORGE (*suddenly gloomy*). Perhaps they don't need soothing.

MYRA. Do yours ?

GEORGE (*avoiding her eyes*). Sometimes . . .

MYRA (*interested and unsuspecting*). Go on ?

GEORGE. A chap gets . . . worried, sometimes—

MYRA. Have you been getting your sums wrong at the office ?

GEORGE. No—of course not.

MYRA. Oh, snap out of it. It can't be very important—you haven't got enough responsibilities for that.

GEORGE (*revealing inner torment*). That's just it—sometimes a chap *wants* responsibilities.

MYRA. What the hell are you talking about ?

GEORGE. Do you want me to tell you ?

MYRA (*nervously, as the truth dawns*). I'm going to chuck this fag away —d'you mind ?

GEORGE (*gravely*). Give it to me.

(MYRA *gives it to him and, with bated breath, watches him carefully stub it out, put it in his pocket case and then put the latter in his breast pocket, reverently, next to his heart.*)

MYRA (*giggling*). What did you do that for ?

GEORGE. Do you *really* want to know ?

MYRA. I—I don't care whether you tell me or not.

GEORGE. Well, I'm going to . . . Myra—

MYRA (*looking out into the street*). Gosh, a car's stopping outside—

GEORGE. Myra—

MYRA (*in excitement*). It's Mr. Neilson—and that's Phyl getting out of it ! (*Pushing him aside and calling out.*) Hallo ! Are you coming in ?

PHYL (*from outside*). Are you alone in the house ?

MYRA. Yes. Hallo, Mr. Neilson !

JOHN. Hallo, Myra !

PHYL. Let us in.

MYRA. Yes, *sir* !

(She dashes out to the front door.)

GEORGE (*at the window*). Good evening, Phyllis. (*He climbs out of the window.*)

PHYL (*outside*). Hallo, Pie-Face.

JOHN (*outside*). Good evening—er—Pie-Face.

George. Good evening, sir.

Phyl.   Why don't you come in for a minute, Pie-Face ?   Come on John . . .

Myra (*to* George).   Yes, you can come in now—it's all right.   Wipe your feet.

(George *disappears from outside the window.*   Phyllis *and* John *enter the room followed by* Myra.   Phyllis *and* John *are in evening dress.   In spite of her regalia there is an utter lack of sophistication about* Phyllis. *Her outfit is cheap, but, within its limits, in perfect taste.   It emphasises her quality of freshness.   She wears a short fur cloak—white, like her dress—and she throws this down on the chair* R. *of the door as she enters* John *comes down* C. *and crosses to the fire.*   Myra *comes to the table.*)

Phyl (*excitedly*).   Now, Myra, is everybody where they should be ?

Myra.   As far as I know.

Phyl.   Then Ted is rehearsing ?

Myra.   That's the story I got.

Phyl.   And the others are at the theatre ?

Myra.   Definitely.   They paid for the tickets last Monday.

Phyl.   Good.   We're safe until half-past ten at the earliest . . . (*She crosses to* John.)

(*In contrast to her mood of happy exuberance* John *is unsmiling, even a little grim.*   George *enters and comes* C.   Phyllis *draws* John *forward on her* R. *below the settee.*)

Listen, now, Pie-Face—You too, Myra.   John—I mean Mr. Neilson *hasn't been here tonight.   You haven't seen him at all.*

George (*puzzled*).   Yes, but he's over there—

Phyl (*firmly*).   *You haven't seen him.   I came back alone*—Understand ?

Myra.   That's okay by me.

Phyl (*sternly.*)   Cut your throats ?

Myra
George } (*together*).   Cut my throat.   (*They suit the action to the words.*)

(Phyllis *does a happy little dance down* R.)

Myra.   Phyl.—you're tiddly.

Phyl (*stopping at once*).   I'm not.   (*She moves up* R. *of the table :* anxiously.)   Do I look it ?

Myra.   You look as whiffled as an owl.

Phyl.   Oh, crikey !   How can you tell ?

Myra.   You look as though you're going to bawl " Knees up, Mother Brown " at any minute.

PHYL. I had some champagne—You mustn't mention that either.

MYRA   }(together) {Okay.
GEORGE   {I won't.

PHYL. What are you going to do now ?

MYRA. We haven't decided yet.

GEORGE (*eagerly*). I brought some duets round—

PHYL. Fine ! Go along, Myra. We shan't interrupt you.

MYRA. We could play four-handed bezique, Mr. Neilson ?

PHYL. No. You two go and play four-handed Stephen Heller.

MYRA (*cuttingly*). I asked Mr. Neilson.

JOHN. I think perhaps a little Stephen Heller . . .

GEORGE. I didn't bring any of the Stephen Heller ones.

JOHN. My taste is catholic—so long as it's a piano duet.

MYRA. I understand. Come on, Pie-Face. I'll take the treble—it's nearer the fire. And for Pete's sake keep your elbows in . . .

(GEORGE *goes out*, MYRA *follows and the door closes behind them*.)

PHYL (*crossing to the back of the settee*). Give me your scarf. (*Taking it and putting it on the chair* R. *of door*.) Now you're my guest for a change. (*She closes the curtains*.)

JOHN (*hesitantly*). I ought not to stay—

PHYL. It's perfectly safe ! You're going to have a drink—I *think*—so no argument . . . (*She looks in the sideboard, up stage cupboard*). Phew ! Thank goodness there's some whisky and soda . . . (*She brings the bottle with siphon and glass to the table, and pours out whisky*.)

(JOHN *crosses to* L. *of the table*.)

You have to say when . . . (*Siphoning*.)

JOHN. When. Thank you—(*taking the glass*.)

(PHYLLIS *replaces the bottle and siphon in the sideboard cupboard*.)

Do I drink alone ?

PHYL. You do !

JOHN. Then you are tiddly !

PHYL. Not wobbly-tiddly, just very bucked. (*She crosses to the settee*.) Oh, John, it's been such a lovely evening . . . It's always fun being with you, John, but tonight has been special—going to your flat—seeing where you live and how you live. I've been longing to do that !

JOHN (*subdued*). You like my flat ? (*He stands with his back to the chair* L. *of the table*.)

PHYL. Oh, it was heavenly. And the dinner—gosh ! And no washing-up to do at the end of it !

(MYRA *and* GEORGE *burst forth with their rendering of "Zampa" in the next room.*)

JOHN. What on earth is that ?

PHYL. The music I provide for my guests ! (*Throwing herself on the settee, with hands stretched above her head.*) Oh, isn't life—*beautiful* !

JOHN. Because of the music !

PHYL. No, silly ! Because of exciting evenings like this ! Because of—oh—because of our meeting in the first place, and the way we laugh at the same silly jokes or just keep silent if we feel like it. Oh, John, we do get on well together, don't we ?

JOHN. Yes . . .

PHYL (*rising hurriedly*). Oh, lord . . . John—please don't think I'm throwing myself at you. You—you don't think that, do you ?

JOHN. Phyl, of course not.

PHYL (*earnestly*). And while we're on the subject, I would like you to tell me, please, when you want to stop taking me out . . . It'd be dreadful if you didn't tell me . . . .

JOHN (*making a slight move to C.*). I'll tell you.

PHYL. John—promise.

JOHN. Promise.

PHYL. Good. And, of course, I'll tell you when *I* get bored ! (*Laughing involuntarily.*)

(JOHN *finishes his drink, turns and puts the glass on the table.*)

JOHN. I think I ought to go now—

PHYL (*blankly*). Oh . . . (*And then, quite happily.*) An appointment or something—

JOHN. Yes—er—no . . . It's amazing ; I can't even tell you a little lie like that ! (*Simply.*) I'm just going, Phyl—that's all.

PHYL (*slowly*). Oh . . . I see . . . (*She manages a smile.*) Thank you for everything, John. I shall always be grateful to you. Good-bye . . . (*Holding out her hand.*)

JOHN (*coming to the R. end of the settee*). No. This is not good enough. There's something I want to tell you, Phyl. It's not going to be easy—

PHYL. Would another drink help ?

JOHN. No—no. Phyl, I'm going to start by trying to excuse myself . . . You know my marriage was not a success ; well—neither was my father's and mother's.　That gives you some idea of my background.　In the circles I've moved in all my life love is a kind of sport, marriage just a social event.　They merely give a bit of spice to life which is otherwise smart and brittle and nothing else.　Can you imagine what that does to you ?

PHYL.　I think you must have been very unhappy . . .

JOHN.　I didn't know what I was missing . . . until tonight.　But let me go back a month—to the time I first saw you—(*He turns away and moves above the table.*)

PHYL.　Three weeks, John.

JOHN (*at the chair above the table*).　No.　I first saw you a week before that—at Arthur's office.　You were waiting for him.　I made up my mind to get to know you through him.　So when I found out he was keen to go abroad I got him this job in Nigeria.　You know the result : I came here to discuss it and we met . . .

PHYL (*astonished*).　Now clever of you !

JOHN (*heavily*).　No, not really.　(*He crosses to the R. end of the settee.*) Ever since then—this is the part that's so hard to tell you—ever since then I've aimed only at one thing : to get you alone in my flat . . .

PHYL.　Oh . . . (*She turns away, much disturbed*).　That's rather—frightening . . .　I wish you hadn't told me . . .

JOHN.　I didn't want to, but I felt I must.　I couldn't go away letting you think that I *wanted* our friendship to finish.

PHYL.　You're going away because it hasn't all ended as you wanted it to end ?

JOHN (*helplessly*).　Phyl, I simply can't trust myself with you , . .

PHYL.　Is that why you insisted on bringing me home tonight ?

JOHN.　Yes.

PHYL.　Then it was me you were thinking of ?

JOHN (*moving above the R. end of the settee and taking her hand*).　Yes.　I suddenly stopped thinking of myself and saw you for the first time as you really are—all sweetness and innocence.　You believed in the sort of person I was pretending to be—

PHYL (*with spirit*).　Sweet and innocent !　Oh, John, anybody'd think I was a—a sort of soppy village maiden who believed everything the squire told her . . . .

JOHN.　Let me put it in another way—(*He moves away R.*)

PHYL.　Yes, I think you'd better.　(*But she smiles.*)

JOHN.　It's just that I saw you as you really are ; a real person—honest, and expecting honesty from me ; a person who sets the right values on things, which I have always treated lightly.　You couldn't be anything else of course, because you live among real people. The Hapgoods and their home are much more important in this world than I am. I've learnt a lot from you, Phyl. I know now what it's like to have trust and comradeship. That's something new for me. (*He turns to her.*) It's been very . . . *warming*—and it's made me feel a finer person than I really am. That is why I'm so ashamed . . . (*He crosses to her.*) Phyl, I realise that what I've told you has ruined everything between us, but one day perhaps you'll forgive me. Will you tell me when that happens—because I shall come straight back to tell you how much I love you—and to ask you to marry me.

PHYL (*rising and moving to the fire wonderingly*). Marry you . . .? I'm just Phyllis Hapgood, and I live in Streatham with all the other Hapgoods. We're ordinary and noisy and we call lunch " dinner" and dinner " tea " and we—

JOHN (*moving to her*). Is that all you're worrying about ?

PHYL. Isn't that enough ?

JOHN (*bursting out*). But—good lord ! Phyl, my darling, if only you'll marry me we'll call supper "breakfast" and have a brass band in every room—I don't care—(*Going to take her in his arms.*)

PHYL (*holding back*). No, wait. We must talk this out. It's important—

JOHN. Can you forgive me for what I've done ?

PHYL. Well, of course !

JOHN. Then—do you love me ?

PHYL. Oh, darling—yes. But we must—(*weakly, as he puts his arms round her*) oh, dear . . .

(JOHN *is about to kiss her when there is a tap at the door. They spring apart and* JOHN *hurriedly crosses down* R.)

Come in, Myra, you idiot.

(MYRA *enters and comes* C.)

Since when have you started knocking at doors ?

MYRA. Since this evening. Now ask me why.

PHYL. I'm not interested in your thought processes. What do you want ?

MYRA (*primly*). I simply came in to ask Mr. Neilson whether there was anything else he would like us to play.

JOHN (*moving up* R.). That's awfully kind of you. Er—have you got a little thing called Zampa ?

MYRA (*coldly*). That, Mr. Neilson, is what we have just played.

JOHN (*confused*). Oh, have you ? I'm sorry . . . Well, what else have you got ?

MYRA. Poet and Pheasant, Cloches de Corneville, H.M.S. Pinafore, Coq d'Or Suite, excerpts from Faust—and we'd do the Battle of Prague at half-speed—

PHYL. Work your way through the lot, Myra. John loves music, I know—

MYRA (*cuttingly*). He doesn't seem to recognise the classics when he hears them.

PHYL. Start with Poet and Peasant. I'll soon let you know when we begin to feel the strain.

MYRA. Another crack like that and you'll get the Battle of Prague at full speed. Is Poet and Pheasant all right with you, Mr. Neilson?

JOHN. Perfectly.

MYRA. We may have a copy of Lieberstraum . . .

PHYL (*shortly*). Poet and Peasant.

MYRA (*nodding*). Poet and Pheasant.

(*She goes out. As soon as the door closes* JOHN *and* PHYLLIS *hurry towards each other.* MYRA *comes back. With great presence of mind* JOHN *changes his direction and goes to his empty glass of whisky, while* PHYLLIS *with equal skill, veers off towards her handbag. They occupy themselves with these objects while* MYRA, *in dead silence, goes to the window seat, collects her bag of sweets and, after giving them a leering grin of infinite meaning, goes out once more.* JOHN *and* PHYLLIS *at once come together.*)

JOHN. Oh, Phyl . . .

(*They kiss.*)

PHYL. John, darling . . .

JOHN (*stroking her hair*). It should have been Lieberstraum.

PHYL. Love's Dream . . . Yes, it should have been . . .

JOHN. I can't believe it.

PHYL. What ?

JOHN. You will marry me ?

PHYL. John, are you quite sure Phyllis Hapgood can make you happy ?

JOHN. She is the only person in the whole world who can.

PHYL. I can only give you my love.

JOHN. *Only* your love !

PHYL. I can give you children as well, of course. Yes, I can do that, darling, if you want children ?

(*They wander across below the table R.*)

JOHN. I want four ! *We'll* have a daughter who gets black eyes at hockey, and a son with hair stinking of violet oil ; another son with romantic ideas of seeing the world—and a child like you . . . What enormous fun your father must have with a family like that ! (*He turns and faces her.*) Oh, Phyl, Phyl . . . Yes, life is beautiful . . . Darling, is there a catch somewhere ? Will your people mind me taking you away ? We shall have to live mostly in Norway, you know.

PHYL (*worried*). That might be a catch . . .

JOHN. Let's deal with it tonight. We'll wait here until they come back.

PHYL (*still worried with her thoughts*). No, John. Let's have tonight to ourselves. I'd like it to be free of any—difficulties. (*She breaks away and goes up C. to the chair R. of the door.*)

(JOHN *goes up R. above the table.*)

We'll go for a long walk together. I want you to tell me about Norway and your house outside Oslo ; the colour of the sea and sky—(*She hands JOHN his scarf.*)

(*She stops short, listening at the door, and then suddenly throws it open, standing L. of the door. MYRA and GEORGE fall sprawling into the room.*)

Myra—what on earth are you doing ?

MYRA (*getting up embarrassed*). Doing up my shoe.

PHYL (*picking up her cloak*). John and I are going.

MYRA. Where to ?

PHYL. We are going skating on the Serpentine.

(JOHN *crosses to PHYLLIS.*)

GEORGE (*still lying in the doorway*). Cheerio, Phyl.

MYRA. So long, Mr. Neilson.

JOHN. Cheerio, Pie—er—Mr.—

GEORGE. Harris. Good night, sir.

(PHYLLIS *and* JOHN *go out. The front door slams.*)

GEORGE. They haven't taken their skates.

(MYRA *goes up to the window and looks out then comes to L. of the table. GEORGE to his feet, collecting his bowler hat and music.*)

MYRA. Oh, ho ! If something isn't hotting up for something my name isn't Myra Hapgood . . . But isn't Mr. Neilson *beautiful* . . (GEORGE *can think of no reply.*) He smells so nice. He's sort of— perfect. (*She studies George and goes to him.*) Pie-Face, why don't you brush that quiff thing down—and keep your mouth closed when you're not speaking ?

GEORGE (*humbly*).   I will if you want me to.

MYRA (*irritably*).   Oh, you make me tired sometimes, the way you always agree with me.   Why don't you try and be a bit more exciting ?   (*She moves below the settee.*)

(GEORGE *shuffles unhappily, conscious of hopeless shortcomings.*)

Look at you standing there as though you couldn't say " Boo " to a goose—

GEORGE.   I've never wanted to say " Boo " to a goose.

MYRA.   Oh, bother it.   Sorry, Pie-Face.   You're all right.   Gosh, I'm a beast.   (*She sits on the settee.*)

GEORGE (*coming to the R. end of the settee*).   No you're not.   You're not a beast at all, Myra.

MYRA.   Yes I am.   You're not so bad really.

GEORGE (*eagerly*).   Well, look here, Myra, I reckon you're an absolute knockout.   I reckon you're jolly pretty—

MYRA.   You mustn't talk like this without a chaperone in the house.

GEORGE (*with sudden awful violence*).   Blast the chaperone !   I'm going to—to—kiss you . . .   (*His courage ebbing.*)   May I, please . . . ?

MYRA (*thoroughly exasperated*).   There—that's you all over !   Don't ask me, you fool.   Do it.   (*She kneels on the settee facing him.*)

(GEORGE *kisses her but bosses his shot in his excitement.*)

Ow !   My nose !   Now you've made my eyes water.

(*But now* GEORGE *is roused.   He seizes* MYRA *and kisses her with instinctive adequacy.   It is more like a rugger tackle than an embrace and he drops his hat and music.*)

Pie-Face—!   (*He kisses her again.   She tears herself free.*)   George Harris, I'll never speak to you again !

GEORGE (*not confidently*).   Oh, yes you will.   (*He picks up his hat and music.*)

MYRA.   Well !   (*She gets off the settee.*)

GEORGE (*right in the depths now*).   I'm sorry, then . . .

MYRA.   Now you can just go home.

GEORGE.   I won't do it again, I promise.

MYRA (*sternly ; looking out front*).   I'll think the matter over.

(GEORGE *sees* MYRA *has not relented and starts towards the door.   Halfway there he stops, half turns and raises his hat.*)

GEORGE.   Good evening.

(*He goes out and closes the door. MYRA bites her nails for a moment then rubs her nose tenderly. Suddenly she sniggers, runs to the window, throws it up and calls.*)

MYRA. Pie-Face !

(*The door immediately opens and GEORGE'S head appears round it.*)

GEORGE (*eagerly*). Did you want me ?

MYRA. You lunatic ! (*She goes to him.*) You meant that, didn't you ? You're sorry, aren't you ?

GEORGE. Yes.

MYRA. Well, then—(*she kisses him.*)

GEORGE. Oh, crikey !

(*He goes to seize her, but MYRA pushes him out of the door, then runs to the window and waves to him as he goes.*)

MYRA. Good-bye ! Good-bye . . .

CURTAIN.

SCENE 2.

SCENE—*The Same. The following evening. Sunday. After church time.*

MR. HAPGOOD *is alone, seated in the chair above the table mending the clock from the mantelpiece. His tools are a screwdriver, an oil can and a pocket knife. The door is open. The repairs proceed for a short while and then he sets the hands and listens. The clock strikes five. He pats it affectionately. The key turns in the lock of the front door and voices are heard in the hall.*

MRS. HAP (*from the hall*). Hallo, Billy. (*She enters, dressed as from out of doors and looks listless and depressed. She comes down and kisses him on the cheek.*)

MR. HAP. Hallo, dear. You back ? Nice service ?

MRS. HAP. Yes.

MR. HAP. Who preached ?

MRS. HAP. The curate.

MR. HAP. H'm. Did you sleep well ?

(*Having no spirit for his banter, MRS. HAPGOOD goes out again without replying. His eyes follow her sadly as she goes off L. TED enters and comes to L. of* MR. HAPGOOD *to watch the repairs.*)

TED.   Done it ?

MR. HAP (*not without pride*).   Yes.   *And* it chimes.   Look, I'll put the hands to six o'clock.   (*Moving the hands round.*)   Now listen . .   (*The clock strikes " three " and then stops.*)   There you are !

TED   (*sarcastically*).   Magnificent !

MR. HAP (*hastily*).   I simply said it chimes.   I always said it would, in spite of general opposition.   It was just a question of studying the innards.

TED.   And you've been doing that for the last ten years.   All you want to do now is to go into the little question of making the ruddy thing strike the *right time*.

MR. HAP.   It only needs a little addition sum.   You simply add three to the number of chimes—

TED.   —or subtract nine.

MR. HAP.   No, that's no good.

TED.   Of course it is.

MR. HAP (*troubled*).   No.   Supposing it strikes five—you can't subtract nine from five.

TED.   You can if you add twelve first.   Five and twelve is seventeen, minus nine is eight.   Gives the same answer.

(MR. HAPGOOD *tries to follow the reasoning.*)

MR. HAP (*with dignity*).   I'll have another go at it next Sunday.   (*He takes the clock back to the mantelpiece.*)   Where's Myra ?

TED.   Walking home with Pie-Face.

MR. HAP.   " Walking Home with Pie-Face "—sounds like a song title !   (*He crosses to the table for the tools.*)

(ARTHUR *enters.*)

TED.   Yes !   (*To* ARTHUR.)   Come and play darts ?

ARTHUR.   No thanks.   (*He sits on the settee, R. end.*)

TED.   Have a game, Dad ?

MR. HAP.   Not tonight, Ted.   (*He crosses to the fireplace.*)

TED.   Well, let's do *something* to cheer ourselves up.   I don't see why we should go about the place moping just because White Cargo is off to Darkest Africa tomorrow.

(MR. HAPGOOD *puts his tools on the mantelpiece.*)

ARTHUR.   Don't you love me ?

TED.   Yes, duckie, but absence will make my heart grow much fonder. Would you be very upset if I left the room for a while so as to change out of this stiff collar ?

ARTHUR. Not if there was a chance that you'd strangle yourself in it.

TED. Wise guy.

(He exits.)

MR. HAP *(standing with his back to the fire, lighting his pipe).* How was your mother in church ?

ARTHUR. Well, she was either pretending she wasn't weeping or else she was talking brightly about how nicely the choir was singing—or else staring at me as though I was already simmering in a native stew-pot.

MR. HAP *(sighing).* Yes. I know . . .

ARTHUR. Dad, you don't think I'm wrong to go away . . . .?

MR. HAP *(gently).* No, I don't . . . But it might have eased the situation if you hadn't sprung it quite so suddenly.

ARTHUR. My God ! It was difficult enough bringing up the subject at all.

MR. HAP. You and I might have got a bit of judicious propaganda working.

ARTHUR *(unhappily).* I should have told *you* more, perhaps . . .

MR. HAP. You can make it up by writing to her regularly. You will do that ?

ARTHUR. You bet I will.

MR. HAP *(earnestly).* Put all you can into your letters. Write to her—not to me. I shall read them anyway.

ARTHUR *(soberly).* I will. But I'll write one or two to you. I'll send them to your office.

MR. HAP *(eagerly).* Will you ? Short ones will do. It's just so that I can show them to one or two of the fellows at the place where I go for lunch.

ARTHUR *(awkwardly).* Dad, you understand why I'm going, don't you ?

MR. HAP. Of course . . . *(He sits on the settee, L. end.)* Years ago, when I was young, I made up my mind to do what you're doing—

ARTHUR *(surprised).* You did ?

MR. HAP. I wanted to go to Rhodesia. I should have gone if I'd had half a chance. But then I met your mother, and she did me the honour of marrying me. *(Absently.)* She was a lovely girl . . and somehow Africa didn't seem to matter. I did bring the subject up a year or so after we were married, but she wasn't keen. I fancy her mother influenced her—*(With a quick glance at the door.)*

You—er—don't remember your granny, do you ?　If you should get married try and pick an orphan ! . . .　I never thought about it after that, but I remember I was enthusiastic while I had the urge.

Arthur (*curiously*).　Did you ever regret not going ?

Mr. Hap (*firmly*).　No.　Your mother made me very happy—very happy.　And we've had a good time in this house, all of us . . . (*Smiling.*)　Still, it would have been fun to see a coconut growing on it's own tree . . .　I met a man last week who goes out to Calabar quite a lot—That's Nigeria ?

Arthur.　Yes, it's down in the South.

Mr. Hap.　He was telling me that a lot of the slaves that crossed the Atlantic used to be shipped from there.　They'd fetch 'em down the Cross River—men, women and children—and pack them into the boats like so many cattle.　Pretty dreadful—but very interesting.　I could have listened to that chap for hours, but then (*with a grimace expressing his distaste*) he started on about his conquests with the black ladies . . .　(*Casually.*)　I dare say you'll have to mind your step over things like that.　You know—Pink Gins and Black Ladies.　It's a bad combination.

Arthur.　I will, Dad.

Mr. Hap (*hastily*).　Oh, I'm not worried about you.　You've got your head screwed on the right way . . . .　(*He draws at his pipe, finds it has gone out and relights it, making rather a business of it.*)　All the same, they say the heat upsets you a bit . . .　(*Grinning embarrassedly.*)　I suppose I ought to give you a general lecture—like old Polonius !　Silly things, lectures.　I used to prefer the wallopings. . . .　But I've often thought that although Polonius was a tedious old fool he did sum things up rather neatly—I mean that idea about being true to yourself . . .　(*Suddenly.*)　I'm sick of this pipe.　Give me one of your cigarettes.

(Arthur *does so.　He is much affected.　They both light up*.　Mr.
　　　　Hapgood *rises and stands by the fire.*)

Arthur (*glumly*).　I wish mother would try to make it a bit easier—like you do.

Mr. Hap.　Everything will work out, you'll see.　In the meantime we must try and help her ; try and understand and be sympathetic.

Arthur (*stubbornly*).　But she isn't fair—

Mr. Hap (*firmly*).　Your mother is one of the finest women that ever lived.

(Enter Myra.　*She is dressed for church—nicely, and looking rather grown
　　　　up.*　George *follows her in, also in his Sunday best.*)

Myra.　Wotcher, Pops !

GEORGE. Hallo, good evening, Mr. Hapgood.

MYRA (*sitting on the L. edge of the table*). I lugged him in to say farewell to Arthur.

ARTHUR. Oh, good.

GEORGE. I was going to say good-bye when we came out of church, but Myra and I—we got left behind somehow . . .

ARTHUR (*grinning*). Yes, funny how that happened !

(*A pause, while* GEORGE'S *mind rustily works out the graceful words of farewell.*)

MYRA (*encouragingly*). Well, go on—say good-bye.

GEORGE. Yes—er—cheerio—(*offering his hand to* ARTHUR.)

ARTHUR. Well, good-bye, George.

MYRA (*prompting* GEORGE). Wish him " Bon voyage."

GEORGE. What ?—Yes, well, I—hope you have a good journey—

MYRA (*in disgust*). I said " Bon voyage," fathead. (*To the others.*) He does speak a bit of French.

ARTHUR. Thanks, anyway, Pie-Face.

(*They wait expectantly for* GEORGE *to say some more.*)

GEORGE (*hoarsely*). I hope the sea'll keep decent for you . . .

MYRA (*translating*). You know—calm.

ARTHUR. I hope it will.

GEORGE (*brilliantly*). They say it gets a bit rough-ish in the Bay—

MYRA (*sharply*). What bay ?

GEORGE (*faltering*). What Bay ? The Bay of Biscay.

MYRA (*to* ARTHUR). Do you go that way ?

ARTHUR. Yes.

MYRA (*nodding, satisfied*). Okay. (*To* GEORGE.) Carry on.

(GEORGE, *who has put his bowler on the arm of the settee, now attempts to assume an air of masterful ease by leaning nonchalantly forward on it— and the bowler suffers. He punches it out.*)

GEORGE. You don't want to feed the fishes, do you ?

ARTHUR. No, I don't !

GEORGE (*inspired*). A chap told me green apples were a jolly good thing—

MYRA (*suspiciously*). What for ?

GEORGE (*uneasily*). Sea-sickness.

MYRA. Don't they give you the belly-ache ?

GEORGE.　I—I expect so ....

MYRA (*jumping off the table* ; *exploding*).　Well, what's the good of that !　Pie-Face, be your age, you twirp . . . Have you finished ?

MR. HAP (*mildly*).　Wouldn't it be a good idea if George said good-bye in his own way ?

(*Enter* MRS. HAPGOOD.　*She crosses above the table and comes down R. to the work box.*)

MRS. HAP.　Ah, there you are, Myra.　I'm glad you came straight back.　Go and take your things off, dear.　(*She takes some work.*)

MYRA.　But I'm going out with Pie-Face.

MRS. HAP (*pained*).　On Arthur's last night ?　(*She sits R. of the table.*)

MYRA.　Why not ?

MRS. HAP.　He's your own brother.　Don't you realise he's going thousands of miles away tomorrow ?　Don't you feel you *want* to stay in ?

MYRA.　Good lord, no !　I feel more like giving three hearty cheers !

ARTHUR (*grinning*).　Let her go, mother.　I'll bear up.

MRS. HAP (*bitterly*).　I cannot understand you children.　Anybody would think you were casual acquaintances instead of brother and sister.　There doesn't seem to be a shred of feeling between you.

MYRA (*with excrutiating melodrama*).　Arthur, my own dear brother— must you go, knowing the broken heart you leave behind ?　Ah, life will be barren when that dee-ar face is no longer—

MR. HAP.　Shut up, Myra.

ARTHUR (*suppressing his laughter*).　Silly little fool.

MRS. HAP (*heavily*).　Go for your walk, Myra.

MYRA.　Come along, Pie-Face.

GEORGE (*to* ARTHUR).　Well, I'll wish you—

MYRA (*dragging him away by the coat tails*).　Oh, don't start that all over again.

(*Exit* MYRA *and* GEORGE.　MR. HAPGOOD *has picked up a book from the settee and is standing with his back to the fire glancing through it.*)

MRS. HAP (*bitterly*).　Well, that reduces us to four.　So much for our loyalty to each other.

MR. HAP.　Don't you think, my dear, that there's something to be said for carrying on as usual ?

MRS. HAP.　You don't understand.　I wanted us all to be here tonight. It would have given us a memory . . .

(ARTHUR *crosses to the gramophone and opens the lid.*)

No, Arthur, please—no music.

(ARTHUR *closes the lid.*)

Whereabouts will you be this time tomorrow ?

ARTHUR (*crossing to the window*). Let's talk about something cheerful, shall we ?

MRS. HAP (*coldly*). Do you mind answering my question ?

ARTHUR. Somewhere in the Irish Sea, I suppose.

(*There is silence.* ARTHUR *stifles a yawn.*)

MRS. HAP (*acidly*). Won't it be nice not to be bored ?

ARTHUR. Sorry—I'm a bit tired.

MRS. HAP. Perhaps if you'd explained earlier that you found your home dull we should have understood each other better—

ARTHUR (*coming to the back of the chair above the table ; angrily*). Look here, mother, it's about time you realised that the deed has been done, and that nothing you can do or say is going to alter it. If we're going to have a row on my last night—

MRS. HAP (*furiously*). How dare you talk to me in this way !

ARTHUR. There shouldn't be any need for what I'm saying—

MR. HAP (*closing his book with a snap ; quietly and authoritatively*). Let's drop the discussion, shall we ? (*He puts the book on the settee.*)

MRS. HAP (*to* ARTHUR). I would never have believed you could be so hard.

(ARTHUR *does not answer, nor even look at her. He crosses to the settee and sits.* TED *enters. He has changed his collar and put on a blazer.*)

TED (*sensing the atmosphere*). What's the joke ?

(*They continue to look grim and ignore him.*)

All right—try this one. There are two deaf chaps in a train. It comes to a station. One chap says to the other : " Is this Wembley ? " The other chap says : " No, Thursday." So the first chap says : " So am I. Let's get out and have a drink . . ." Ha, ha, ha !

(*They continue to ignore him.*)

All right—let it go. (*He crosses to the gramophone.*)

MR. HAP. No, Ted. No.

(*The front door bell rings.*)

TED (*clicking his tongue disapprovingly*). Don't they know there's been a death in the house ?

(*He goes out to answer the door. Nobody speaks.* PHYLLIS *enters, followed by* JOHN. *The unexpectedness of* JOHN'S *appearance takes them all by surprise.* TED *takes* JOHN'S *hat and exits, going off* L.)

PHYL. Hallo—

ARTHUR. Hallo !

PHYL. Hallo, mother . . . Mother, I've brought a visitor.

JOHN. Good evening.

MR. HAP. Good evening, Mr. Neilson.

(ARTHUR *rises.*)

PHYL (*indicating the door*). Arthur, be a sport, will you, please . . . (*She is R.C. by the table.*)

ARTHUR (*going to the door*). Yes, all right.

JOHN. Just a minute, Arthur. Did they tell you about your quinine ?

ARTHUR. Yes, I've started already.

JOHN. Good. I'll see you later.

(*Exit* ARTHUR. *He closes the door.*)

MR. HAP. Won't you sit down, Mr. Neilson ?

(JOHN *sits on the settee.*)

PHYL. Dad, John and I—

MRS. HAP. " John " ?

PHYL. Yes, mother . . . We—John has asked me to marry him.

(*There is dead silence.*)

JOHN. This is in the nature of a formal request for your approval.

MR. HAP (*carefully, to* PHYLLIS). Well, this is a bit of a surprise. Your mother and I had no idea you'd even been meeting each other—

PHYL. We've met every day. We know each other very well.

MRS. HAP. In three weeks ?

PHYL. John is the sort of person you can get to know very well in three days if you want to.

MRS. HAP. And you wanted to . . . ?

PHYL. Yes, mother. We love each other.

MR. HAP. This is all rather a bombshell, you know—

JOHN. I'm afraid that is my fault. I know it's a bit sudden, but you see, I have to go back to Norway next month.

MRS. HAP. Norway ! For how long ?

JOHN. I shall be there for at least eighteen months.

MRS. HAP.   And you want to take Phyllis with you ?

JOHN.   Yes. I do.

MR. HAP.   You'd live in England after that, of course ?

JOHN.   My home is in Oslo.   I was born in Norway—I've lived there most of my life. . All my interests and my friends are there.   I live in London about three months of the year—My job brings me here.

(Another silence.)

PHYL.   You see, mother, it isn't as though we were going away for good.   We shall be back once every year.

MRS. HAP (*painfully*).   I suppose Mr. Neilson has told you all about himself—about his way of living—his . . . divorce ?

PHYL.   All I want to know.

MRS. HAP.   You'll realise that your father and I can't be easy in our minds.   Once a man has been married and divorced . . .

PHYL.   Oh, but mother—as though a thing like that mattered—in these days !

JOHN.   No, please, Phyl.   I'd like a chance to explain.

PHYL.   Very well, darling.   (*She turns up stage a little.*)

JOHN.   Frankly I had no idea divorce was so distressing—for those outside the two parties concerned.   I mean.   Though it was unpleasant enough for Pauline and me . . .

PHYL (*coming down a little C.*).   There's no need to go into all that, John.   I'm glad you divorced her—glad you had the courage.

JOHN.   Believe me, Mrs. Hapgood, my first marriage couldn't have worked.   I misread my wife's character.   I stood by her until— until she asked me for grounds for divorce.

MRS. HAP.   And what makes you think you're not misreading— your own word—Phyl's character now ?

JOHN.   I'm older and wiser.   I couldn't make the same mistake twice.

MR. HAP.   Suppose we accept your explanation—suppose my wife and I put aside our dislike for the idea. of Phyllis marrying a divorced man—do you think that a girl brought up as Phyllis has been brought up is the right wife for a man of your means—a man of your way of living ?

JOHN.   I should have thought that was a question only Phyllis could answer.

MRS. HAP.   Phyllis is a child.   I'm her mother.   I know her better than she knows herself. . . .   Your outlooks are different.

JOHN.   They were different.   I'm not so sure we think so very differently about things now—about the things that would affect our lives together. . . . I must confess that I had started all wrong with Phyllis—

PHYL. Please, John—it isn't necessary. My mother wouldn't understand. She doesn't want to.

MR. HAP. Hadn't you better let Mr. Neilson say what he wants to ?

JOHN. I'd like to, Phyl.

PHYL. All right.

JOHN. I first came to this house with the intention of meeting Phyllis, not to talk to you about a job for Arthur. I happened to see her and Arthur together in London, and I simply used Arthur as a means of meeting his sister. He knew nothing about this, of course.

MRS. HAP (*sarcastically*). Love at first sight?

JOHN. No—not love—not then.

MRS. HAP. Then what you're telling us is that you tricked your way into this house just to . . . seduce Phyllis ?

JOHN. It sounds pretty unpleasant, but—

PHYL (*moving in to the table*). Mother, he needn't have explained all this. It wasn't necessary.

MRS. HAP. I'm glad I know. I might have been weak and stupid enough to have given way against all my instincts.

PHYL. John has told you because he wanted to put himself right with you and Daddy—to start off honestly—and all you can say—

MRS. HAP (*rising*). It was a mean, dirty trick.

PHYL. Well, of course it was—but he discovered he couldn't go through with it.

MRS. HAP. Billy, I don't want her to marry him. I don't think he's the right man for her. (*She goes to work-box down* R.)

PHYL (*her voice rising*). I'm going to marry John.

MR. HAP. We'd better talk this over *quietly*—

MRS. HAP (*turning and moving to back of the chair* R. *of the table ; tensely*). Nothing will make me change my mind. Forgive me, Mr. Neilson, but Phyllis is my daughter. However it hurts you and her for the moment I've got to say that your behaviour has been unforgivable. To have cheated your way into this house as you have done—

PHYL. Mother, please—

MRS. HAP. Be quiet, Phyllis !

PHYL (*angrily*). I won't be quiet. John has been wonderful—absolutely honest—and all he's got is abuse. I love him and that's all there is to be said. (*Crossing to* JOHN.) John, I'll marry you as soon as possible.

Mr. Hap. Phyl, dear, steady . . .   There's something in what your mother says.   There are two sides to this question.   I know how you feel ; you love him.   It's wonderful being in love—nothing else seems to matter.   But we should think it all over quietly. That isn't an unreasonable thing to suggest.   Don't you think it would be best if you didn't see each other for three or four months, and then at the end of that time, having looked at the thing calmly and quietly—

Phyl. But John will be in Norway.

Mr. Hap (*gently*). You might decide not to marry him, you know.

Phyl. You're wrong.   No, Daddy, I don't see the point of waiting. You were right just now—Nothing else does matter—

Mrs. Hap (*moving above the table*). I see !   I don't matter—your father doesn't matter !   Nothing matters but this infatuation.   You're behaving like a stupid schoolgirl, and as far as I'm concerned, I will never give my consent.

Phyl (*facing her*). Nothing is going to stop me.

Mrs. Hap. You realise what you are saying, don't you ?   You know what it means ?

Phyl. If it means I'm finished with home—yes, I know.

Mrs. Hap. Then there's no point in saying any more . . .   (*She breaks R. to the sideboard and stands with her back to the room.*)

Phyl. Very well, I'll go now. . . . (*To* John.)   I'll go and put a few things together.   I won't be a minute.

(*She exits, leaving the door open.   There is a painful pause.*)

John (*rising*). I'm—sorry, sir . . .

Mr. Hap. But where are you going to take her until you're married ?

John. I'd like to think you're going to trust me.   I'll take her anywhere you'd like to suggest.

Mr. Hap. My sister—she'll look after her.   Yes, take her there, please.   Phyllis will tell you where she lives.

John. I'll see she goes there. (*Turning to* Mrs. Hapgood.)   Mrs. Hapgood, I—

Mr. Hap. Don't say any more, please.   Just leave it at that.

(John *exits into the hall, takes his hat and gloves from the stand and goes off R.   Arthur enters from off L.*)

Arthur. What on earth has happened ?   Phyl rushed upstairs like a tornado.   What's the matter ?

Mr. Hap. You might as well know.   She's going with Neilson.

Arthur. You mean—to be married ?

Mr. Hap. Yes.

Mrs. Hap (*to* Arthur).   So that is two of you going . . .

(Arthur *does not answer.*)

Isn't it ?

Arthur (*uncomfortably*).   Yes . . . I suppose it is.

Mrs. Hap.   Is that all you have to say ?

Arthur.   What else can I say ?

Mrs. Hap (*in a hard voice*).   You might say that you were sorry you ever brought that man here ; that you were wrong to go to Africa—

(*Enter* Phyllis.   *She comes C.*)

Phyl.   Good-bye mother . . .

(Mrs. Hapgood *brushes past her and goes out of the room without making a reply.*)

Mr. Hap.   Go and talk to her, Arthur.   Help her—but don't weaken.

Arthur.   Very well, Dad.   I'll do what I can . . .   (*He moves to* Phyllis.)   Are you really going now, Phyl ?

Phyl.   Yes.

Arthur.   Best of luck.

Phyl.   And to you.

(*They kiss in a brotherly—sisterly fashion.*)

Arthur.   You'll be all right.

(*He exits, leaving the door open and goes off L.*)

Phyl.   I've packed my pyjamas and a toothbrush.   Will you please ask Myra if she'll—

Mr. Hap (*sadly*).   I'll tell her to put everything together.   I'll send it all on as soon as I can.

Phyl.   Thank you . . .   (*Facing him squarely.*)   Are *you* going to say good-bye, Daddy ?

Mr. Hap.   No, dear, I'm not going to say good-bye ; that sounds too final.   I'll say au revoir if you like, because I feel sure that one day, please God, all this unhappiness will pass—and who knows, we may find a way of making that day come sooner than we expect.   I know you love him honestly and truly, so try not to be too hurt by anything your mother may have said.   After all, dear, she knows very little about him.   Neither do I for that matter, and it came as a bit of a shock to us. . . .   Anyway, it's no good saying any more.   It'll all come right one day.   And remember, Phyl—your mother loves you ; she loves you very deeply. That should help . . . And as for me—well . . .

(Too overcome to go on. He takes her in his arms, holds her tightly for a moment and then abruptly releases her. PHYLLIS goes, weeping, from the room. She shuts the door. MR. HAPGOOD stares miserably after her, his shoulders sag and he buries his hands deep in his pockets. He looks sadly about him. The clock strikes three. He gives it a crooked smile and crosses to the mantelpiece. It begins to strike again. He lifts it from the mantelpiece and walks slowly across to the table with it and with his screwdriver. It is still chiming as—

The CURTAIN *falls.*

ACT III.

Scene i.

Scene.—*The same. Two years later. An evening in late April.*

A pair of sheets are draped over a chair by the fire, airing. The room is bright with spring flowers, but is unoccupied when the curtain rises. The door is open. The front door bell rings and Ted passes through the hall to answer it.

A Boy's Voice (*off*). Name of 'apgood ? (*He hands Ted a telegram.*)

Ted (*in the hall*). Yes. (*He reads the telegram.*) No answer. (*He closes the front door and wanders in vaguely, sees nobody in the room and throws the telegram on the table. He is looking pale and miserable. He crosses to the window and stares out.*)

(*Enter Myra. She is now nineteen and we notice, as also in Ted's case, the difference that the two years have made in her. She has more poise, her hair is neatly done, her limbs no longer sprawl. She is grown up. But the essential Myra has not changed.*)

Myra. Oh !—It's you, Ted. I thought it was Pie-face. Do you know if he has been ? (*She stands up C.*)

Ted. No.

Myra. He hasn't been or you don't know ?

Ted (*shortly*). I don't know and I don't care.

Myra (*singing and serenading him, melodramatically*). Ah, love, love ! The ecstacy of it !—and yet, ah me !—the bitterness too ! Try a cold bath. (*She comes down to the settee, sits and picks up a paper.*)

Ted (*savagely*). Will you shut up ! (*He goes to the door.*)

Myra. If it wasn't Pie-Face who was it ?

Ted (*shortly*). Telegram from Arthur. You'd better tell them.

(*He indicates the telegram on the table and goes out, turning R. and going out of the front door. Myra rises, crosses to the table, seizes the telegram and reads it. Enter Mrs. Hapgood. She starts to cross R. above the table.*)

Myra (*handing the telegram to Mrs. Hapgood*). It's come, mother ! Now you can sleep happily.

MRS. HAP. Go and tell Dad ! He's upstairs. (*She reads the telegram with great delight.*)

(MYRA *goes no further than the door.*)

MYRA (*bawling up the stairs*). Daddeee ! They've brought the good news from Ghent ! Arthur's on his way !

MRS. HAP. He's at Plymouth now—

MYRA (*bawling to* MR. HAPGOOD). He's at Plymouth now ! (*She goes to her mother, putting an arm round her and reading over her shoulder.*) Do you see what time he gets here ?

MRS. HAP. Oh, what does it matter ? I shan't sleep a wink anyway !

(MYRA *takes the telegram.*)

MYRA. Nobody will if we've got to get his breakfast at five-thirty in the morning !

(*Enter* MR. HAPGOOD.)

MR. HAP. The telegram ? (*He takes it from* MYRA.)

MRS. HAP (*coming down* R.). He's in England ! Think of it !

MYRA (*reading the telegram over* MR. HAPGOOD'S *shoulder*). " Arrived Plymouth stop train due Paddington five-thirty a.m. tomorrow stop whoopee stop don't bother meet me stop love Arthur. That's fourpennyworth of stops. He's mad !

MR. HAP. That's fine. Er—shall we " bother meet him " ? (*He puts the telegram on the table.*)

MRS. HAP (*crossing behind the table to the fire*). Of course we will ! I shall slip round to Brown's later and order a taxi. . . . Think of it—he'll be here, in this room—after two years !

MR. HAP (*moving to the sideboard*). Pinching my beer, I expect. (*He opens a bottle of beer.*)

MYRA. And expecting us all to wait on him ! Huh ! I'll tell the Big White Carstairs where he gets off !

MRS. HAP (*feeling the sheets*). No, you must let him down gently. We all must. After all, he's used to black servants.

MYRA. So we all dash up with shining teeth when he claps his hands.

(MR. HAPGOOD *brings his bottle and glass to the table.*)

MRS. HAP. You know very well you're looking forward to seeing him.

MYRA. Depends whether he brings any respectable presents.

MRS. HAP. We mustn't expect them—but I dare say he will. (*She folds up the sheets.*)

MR. HAP. I hear the usual procedure is to pick up something in Madeira. It's very often a carpet made in Leeds. (*He puts the bottle and glass down and sits above the table.*)

MYRA. Arthur will do all his picking-up in London, when he gets here. He'll pick up a skirt.

MRS. HAP. A skirt ? (*She puts the sheets on the R. arm of the settee.*)

MYRA. Young lady to you. She'll be the sort who'll say " Oo ! " and gaze at him awe-struck when he starts putting over those crashing lies he wrote in his letters.

MRS. HAP. I believe every word he wrote. As for him finding a lady friend, that wouldn't surprise me at all. Even Ted has one, and he's only twenty !

MR. HAP. So has George Harris—and he is only twenty-one. . . .

MYRA. Hark at the wit !

MRS. HAP (*taking the chair from in front of the fire and putting it L. of the door*). Does Ted know about the telegram ? (*She crosses down R. to work-box.*)

MYRA. Yes, but he went out. He certainly looked as though he could do with some fresh air.

MRS. HAP. Oh, why ?

MYRA. He was staring out of the window with a face like the one in the advertisement for Syrup of Figs.

MRS. HAP. Oh, its that stupid little love affair. So irritating. But every boy goes through it. So long as she's a nice girl—(*She collects her sewing, moves to the chair R. of the table and sits.*)

MYRA. Dandy is all right. (*She moves to L. of MR. HAPGOOD.*)

MRS. HAP. " Dandy " ! What an absurd name !

MYRA (*putting an arm round MR. HAPGOOD's shoulder*). It's just his name for her. She calls him " Teddy Bear."

MRS. HAP. Myra dear, take those sheets up to Arthur's bed.

MYRA (*crossing to the settee and collecting them*). Right you are. (*She turns at C.*) Look, if Pie-Face turns up would you mind telling him to go to hell ?

MRS. HAP. Well, really !

MYRA. Breaking a date with me. . . .

(*She goes out.*)

MRS. HAP. She expected him at the tennis club this evening.

MR. HAP. Oh, that was it, was it ?

MRS. HAP (*happily*). Billy. I can't get over it . . .

MR. HAP. Arthur ?

MRS. HAP. Yes. I wonder if he has changed at all ?

MR. HAP. In his last letter there was something about growing a moustache . . .

MRS. HAP. Yes, it sounds absurd ! Arthur with a moustache !

MR. HAP (*gently*). Mary.

MRS. HAP. Yes, dear.?

MR. HAP. He'll be going back at the end of his leave . . .

(MRS. HAPGOOD *looks up startled*.)

Will you make it easy for him ?

MRS. HAP (*simply*). Yes.

MR. HAP. You've quite forgiven him ?

MRS. HAP. Forgiven him ! You didn't see the tears in his eyes when he kissed me good-bye. I'm sure at that moment he hated going. And his wonderful letters . . . It's funny, but he's been much closer to me since he's been away. Perhaps for the first time in his life I've really understood him.

MR. HAP. I'm very glad, my dear—very glad. It will be grand to have him home . . . There's something else . . .

MRS. HAP. Not trouble, I hope ?

MR. HAP (*rising*). No. On the contrary. Phyllis and John are back in London. They arrived last week. We all had lunch in town yesterday.

MRS. HAP (*eagerly*). How was she ?

MR. HAP. Fine and radiant—and radiantly happy.

MRS. HAP. I'm glad . . .

(*Pause.*)

MR. HAP. You never told me she'd written to you.

MRS. HAP. It would have done no good . . .

MR. HAP. Perhaps it would. I might have persuaded you to answer her letters.

MRS. HAP. I did. I wrote six letters . . .

MR. HAP (*surprised*). She didn't tell me that.

MRS. HAP. I never posted them.

MR. HAP. You never posted them !

MRS. HAP. No, I—I couldn't bring myself to . . . Then after her third letter I made up my mind if she wrote again I'd send them all together. She never wrote again.

MR. HAP (*coming down to her and putting an arm round her shoulder*). You're a silly, stubborn old darling.

Mrs. Hap.   Perhaps I am.   But she did hurt me very much.   You don't know how much . . .

Mr. Hap.   Who told you that ?   (*He moves back to his chair and sits.*) Now, listen, Mary.   You've got to make up this quarrel.   It's all nonsense . . . now that you're going to be a grandmother—

Mrs. Hap (*slowly*).   What did you say ?

Mr. Hap.   We're going to be grandparents in six months.

Mrs. Hap.   Oh . . .

Mr. Hap.   Can I ask them round tonight ?   Can I, Mary ?

Mrs. Hap (*hurriedly*).   No, not tonight—Let me get used to the idea first.   Let me be sure I can meet her husband without making matters worse.

Mr. Hap.   But Mary—

Mrs. Hap.   She can come alone—I'd like to see her alone.

Mr. Hap.   No. If she comes they both come.

(Myra *comes in.*)

Myra.   Still no Pie-Face ?

Mr. Hap.   Not yet.

Myra.   That lad just doesn't know what he's in for.

Mrs. Hap.   Phyl and her husband are back.

Myra (*excitedly*).   How do you know ?

Mrs. Hap.   Daddy had lunch with them in town yesterday.   She is going to have a baby. . . .

Myra.   And about time too !   (*Eagerly.*)   What are you going to do about it ?

(Mrs. Hapgood *rises and comes down to the work box.   She has her back to the others.*)

Mrs. Hap.   I don't know.

(Myra *studies* Mrs. Hapgood *thoughtfully for a moment.*)

Myra.   Dad, don't you think you need a wash ?

Mr. Hapgood (*surprised*).   No, I'm all right.

(Myra *mimes that she wants to be alone with her mother.   Comprehension dawns on* Mr. Hapgood *and he mimes his understanding.   He rises, picks up his glass and takes a step towards the door, then he turns back to the table, picks up the bottle and moves up to the door.*)

I'll be in the garden, Mrs. H.

(*He goes out and off L.*)

MYRA (*coming L. of the table*).   Well, mother, what are you going to do about it ?

MRS. HAP.   There isn't anything I can do.   (*She returns to her chair and sits.*)

MYRA.   Yes, there is.   You can come with me to see Phyl and her husband—

MRS. HAP.   No, dear—

MYRA.   Why can't you ?

MRS. HAP.   Because little girls don't understand these things.   Wait until *you* are grown up and have children and one of them hurts you more than you can bear—

MYRA.   But that was two years ago.   Phyl loves you, you know she does.   And it's all nonsense to say I wouldn't understand.   I've grown up now.   We all have . . .   (*As she moves above the table to* MRS. HAPGOOD.)   Fancy Phyl with a baby!   And Arthur with a moustache.   The next you'll hear is that Ted's got a beard and I've married a dear old man a in bath chair ! . .   Oh, Mum, we've all had such a good time—and even if we've seemed ungrateful sometimes and made things difficult for you we haven't meant anything.   Phyl didn't.   She just fell in love.

MRS. HAP.   You're a sweet child, Myra. . . .

MYRA.   Now, now, Mummy.

MRS. HAP.   Oh, well—young lady then . . .   Yes, I suppose you'll all be men and women very soon.

MYRA.   And then you and Daddy will have some peace !

MRS. HAP.   Peace—with more babies about !   And yet I suppose the happiest time of my life was when you were all babies. We had very little money, Daddy was only a poorly paid clerk then, and what with money worries and doctors bills and so on— it was a big struggle.   But I didn't mind ; I enjoyed it.   You were all so entirely dependent on me then.   I think that was perhaps the chief reason for my being so happy.

MYRA (*sitting on the table*).   But Mummy, that's all in the past.   You'd be just as happy now, in the present, if you got it all sorted out. We're no longer babies, I know, but you've still got us—in a different way.   Arthur's coming home, Ted and I are still here— and Phyl is just longing for the first opportunity to fling her arms round your neck.   Oh, Mummy, what about it— ?

MRS. HAP.   Well, dear, I—

(*The door bell rings.*)

MYRA.   Damn, that'll be Pie-Face.   I wanted to talk to you more about Phyl.   Would you mind telling him I'm not going to give him an audience tonight ?

Mrs. Hap. Don't be such a baby.

Myra (*going to door*). I'm going to sulk. Tell him I'm out.

Mrs. Hap. I shall do no such thing.

(*The door bell rings again.*)

Myra. I'm not going to let him in. He's a dirty dog.

(*She goes out and off L., leaving the door open.*)

Mrs. Hap (*murmuring*). Silly child . . .

(*She goes out and opens the front door.*)

George (*off*). Evening, Mrs. Hapgood.

Mrs. Hap (*shutting the front door*). Hallo, George. Come in.

(*He comes in. George has developed somewhat in self-confidence during the two years that have elapsed, though this does not become very apparent until after he has declared himself to Myra. For she is still his Achilles' heel.*)

George (*as they both enter, George on the R.*). Is Myra in ?

Mrs. Hap. Yes. But I warn you she's feeling haughty.

George. Oh lord . . . But I couldn't turn up at the club this evening, really.

Mrs. Hap. She's upstairs. We'll try and get her down. (*At the door and calling upstairs.*) Myra, stop being childish. Come down and see George.

Myra (*from above*). I'm busy.

Mrs. Hap (*calling*). But he's got something to tell you—(*Hastily to George.*) Think of something—quickly !

George (*nervously*). But I *have* got something to tell her—some news.

Mrs. Hap (*calling*). There you are, Myra—he's got some news.

Myra (*from above*). It can keep.

George (*calling*). Be a sport, Myra. It's important—

Myra (*from above*). Tell me from there.

Mrs. Hap (*to George*). Keep on like that and she'll come. I'm going into the garden with Daddy.

(*She goes off L.*)

George (*in the doorway, calling*). Myra—

Myra (*from above*). What ?

George (*calling*). I'll explain why I wasn't there if you'll come down.

Myra. Tomorrow will do.

George (*to himself, in despair*). Oh, crikey ! (*Calling.*) Myra—

MYRA (*in a tired voice, from above*).   What ?

GEORGE (*calling*).   I'm going away. . . .

MYRA (*from above, slightly startled*).   Good idea.

GEORGE (*calling*).   There's something else—

MYRA (*from above*).   Tell me when you come back.

GEORGE (*desperately*).   Myra . . . will you marry me . . . ?

MYRA (*faintly, from above*).   W-what did you say . . . ?

GEORGE (*calling*).   Will you marry me ?

MYRA (*breathlessly, from above*).   Wait a minute . . .

(GEORGE *advances downstage to L. of table, running a finger round the inside of his collar*.)

(MYRA *enters, apparently self-possessed*.)

(*Severely*.)   Now, what's all this nonsense ?   (*She is L. of* GEORGE.)

GEORGE (*in a rush*).   It's like this ; I've got a transfer to Cape Town and I asked them if I could take a wife and they said they'd let me know and then I said I wasn't sure about the wife yet so they said well make sure and we'll let you know this end . . . .   But, if you say you'll marry me and then they say I can't take you, I shan't go—because . . . (*hanging his head*) I love you . . .

MYRA (*much affected and saying the first thing that enters her head*).   Why weren't you at the tennis club this evening . . . ?

GEORGE.   It's all to do with this transfer—

MYRA (*moving to the settee*).   You'd better start at the beginning.   (*She sits, R. end*.)

GEORGE (*moving behind the settee*).   The beginning is—will you marry me ?

MYRA (*indignantly*).   You can't come barging in here expecting an answer straight out—Sort of, " What's the time ? "—" Half-past nine."—" Will you marry me ? "—" Sure I will ! "

GEORGE (*eagerly*).   You will ?

MYRA (*hastily*).   That was just an example.   You go on talking while I think.

GEORGE.   They've offered me this transfer to Cape Town.   The salary is good—Four-hundred and twenty.   But it means going away for three years.   That's why I want you and me to get married.   The directors don't like juniors taking wives with them the first time, but old Henshawe—my boss—says he'll try and make 'em agree to it.   I made it pretty plain that I'd prefer to keep my present position if they couldn't see their way to it.

MYRA.   Pie-Face, you idiot !

GEORGE (*crossing to the table soberly*).   No.   I know what I want.   I've
been hanging round here a good number of years now . . .   I'd
have asked you to marry me before only I wasn't earning enough,
and promotion is slow in this country.   Besides, I wasn't sure it was
any good . . .   I haven't got a lot of sparkle, I know.   I mean
I'm not —well, I'm not—

MYRA (*helpfully*).   Not worthy of me ?

GEORGE (*humbly*).   Yes, that's it.

MYRA (*nodding*).   Something in that !

GEORGE (*moving back to the settee*).   Nobody is.   I'm terrible when it
comes to talking . . .   I'm trying to tell you how I think of you.
All I can say is that there's nobody in the whole world that can
touch you . .

MYRA (*profoundly moved*).   I'm not a measle germ !

GEORGE (*ruefully*).   Gosh, you don't help much.   If you'd just *hint*
that you didn't think I was a bit of dirt—

MYRA.   I wouldn't have stuck you all these years if I thought that.

GEORGE (*facing her at the end of the settee, glumly*).   Aren't you going to
say anything else to get me out of this jam.

MYRA (*deliberately*).   No, Pie-Face.   My motto is deeds, not words—

(*She kneels on the arm of the settee and kisses him firmly on the lips.*)

GEORGE (*thunderstruck*).   Crikey . . .

(*They kiss again and sit on the settee.*)

You love me too !

MYRA.   I suppose I do.   That kiss seems to have made all the
difference.

GEORGE (*eagerly*).   Let's have some more—

MYRA (*holding back*).   Let me get my breath back first.

GEORGE.   All right, say when.

MYRA.   We ought to talk—(*She rises and crosses to the table.*)

GEORGE.   I thought your motto was " deeds " !

MYRA.   Aren't I going to marry you ?

GEORGE.   Yes—Gorblessyou.   (*He rises.*)

MYRA.   When will you know if I can come with you ?

GEORGE.   Probably the day after tomorrow.   That's the directors'
meeting. . . .   (*Going to her.*)   Have you got your breath back
yet ?

MYRA (*firmly*).   Business first.   If we go, when will it be ?

GEORGE.   About a month after that.

MYRA. Phew ! That means rushing into matrimony !

GEORGE. Suits me.

MYRA (*excited*). Pie-Face, what fun !

GEORGE. You bet . . . I say—I hope nobody is going to object.

MYRA (*frowning*). They might try and tell us we are too young.

GEORGE. I'm nearly twenty-two. I can take care of you—

MYRA. Chump ! I can take care of myself. Will your people mind ?

GEORGE (*confidently*). No need to worry about them. They like you fine. Er—what about your mother and father ?

MYRA. Don't know. I'll have a talk with Dad.

GEORGE (*ruefully*). I ought to do that, didn't I ?

MYRA. You'd make a mess of it.

GEORGE (*brightening*). I expect I would.

MYRA (*thoughtfully*). Pie-Face—what will your mother say ?

GEORGE. I can give you her exact words. She'll say, " It's *about time* you asked her ! "

MYRA. Won't she be—sad at your leaving home and going abroad ?

GEORGE. There were six of us kids. Her policy has always been—chuck 'em in and see if they can swim . . . Good idea.

MYRA. But she must be fond of you ?

GEORGE. How can she help it !

MYRA (*distraite*). Funny . . .

GEORGE. What !

MYRA. Supposing you and I had a lot of kids, and supposing we brought them up very carefully and loved them—and then they all started disappearing with their wives and husbands and jobs . . . wouldn't it hurt you a little ?

GEORGE. Good Lord, no ! It's a natural thing to happen.

MYRA. It's a moot point.

GEORGE (*exasperated*). Look here, what are we talking about ?

MYRA. It was just a thought.

GEORGE. Well, stop it. Give me another kiss.

MYRA. I don't give kisses. They're taken from me.

GEORGE. That's good enough

(*They kiss again.* GEORGE *sits on the table with her. They face the auditorium their arms round each other.*)

  Myra, I love you like fury . . .

MYRA (*softly*). You're not so bad yourself.

GEORGE.   Are you as bucked as I am ?

MYRA (*happily, laying her head on his shoulder*).   Oh, Pie-Face . . .

(*Their backs being to the door, they do not see* MR. HAPGOOD *enter.   He gives a start of surprise, surveys them for a moment and then coughs gently.* GEORGE *practically falls off the table.*)

MR. HAP.   Good evening, George.

GEORGE.   G-good evening, Mr. Hapgood.

MR. HAP.   I think I left my pipe . . . (*Crossing to the mantlepiece, but not finding the pipe.*)   Oh, there was a message for you, George. Myra said you were to go to hell—

MYRA.   That message is cancelled.   I've thought of a much better one now.

(MRS. HAPGOOD *enters, her husband's pipe in her hand.*)

MRS. HAP.   Here it is, Billy.   You left it on the rockery.   (*She comes down C.*)   Myra, dear, don't sit on the table like that.

MYRA.   Mother, Pie-Face and I want to be engaged—

(MRS. HAPGOOD *sits on the* R. *arm of the settee.*)

We just want you to say whether you have any objections.

MR. HAP.   H'm . . .   Well . . .   We can scarcely say this is a surpise eh, Mary ?

MRS. HAP (*smiling*).   Indeed no, though we didn't expect it quite so soon—

MR. HAP (*easily*).   Oh I think the sooner we accustom ourselves to the idea the more settled we shall all be—especially George ! And what is your financial position, Mr. Harris ?

GEORGE.   Well, it's not so hot at present, but—

MYRA (*interrupting again, and speaking deliberately for* GEORGE'S *benefit*). We don't know yet when we shall get married, but we just thought we'd let you know we were heading for it.

MRS. HAP.   I'm ever so glad, dear.   (*Kissing her.*)   George will make a fine husband for you—when he's able to set up a home for you both. . . .

MR. HAP.   Congratulations, George.

(MYRA *crosses to* MR. HAPGOOD.)

GEORGE.   Thank you, sir.   I reckon I deserve them.

MR. HAP.   You do !   A lesser man would have given up years ago.

GEORGE.   Ah, what I meant was—

MYRA.   All right, we know.   I'm beautiful, virtuous, kind—

GEORGE.   I hadn't thought of " beautiful " !

MYRA.   You rat !

MR. HAP.   That's a fine way to talk to your future husband !

MRS. HAP.   George, I'm so pleased.   (*Kissing him.*)   You've been so patient.   (*She crosses down R. below the table.*)

MR. HAP (*giving* MYRA *a congratulatory kiss*).   Pleased with yourself ?

MYRA.   Yes, he's improved a lot lately.

MR. HAP.   I think you're a lucky girl.

MYRA (*soberly*).   Yes . . .   (*She crosses to* GEORGE. *To* MRS. HAPGOOD.)   We are awfully in love.

MRS. HAP (*warmly*).   Of course you are, dear.

MYRA.   But we know.   It's real.   If it wasn't for his small salary we'd like to marry quite soon. . . .   Wouldn't it be lovely if someone said to Pie-Face " Harris, my boy, you can have a job at . . . four hundred and twenty pounds a year ! " . . .

GEORGE.   Yes, but I—

(MYRA *covertly silences him.*)

MRS. HAP (*smiling indulgently*).   Oh, but you'd wait a year or two, dear, surely ?

MYRA.   What for ?

MRS. HAP.   Why, you're only eighteen—

MYRA.   Nineteen next month . . .   (*Abruptly, to* GEORGE.)   Did you bring your old man's car ?

GEORGE.   Yes, it's outside.

MYRA.   Let's go for a ride.   (*She leads him up C.*)

GEORGE (*returning hesitantly*).   If there's nothing else to talk about—

MYRA.   There isn't.   (*Taking his hand.*)   Come along.

MRS. HAP.   Shall I get a little celebration supper ready ?

MYRA.   Hurray !   Yes !   Something to drink, too.   We shall be thirsty if I know Pie-Face !

MRS. HAP.   Half-past-nine ?

MYRA.   About that—

(GEORGE *and* MYRA *go out and off* R.)

MR. HAP.   I suppose that means we shall soon have to be thinking about a wedding present ?   I wonder if they'd like that clock. . . .

MRS. HAP (*going to the workbox*).   Oh, I dare say it will be some time before he's earning four hundred and twenty pounds a year !

MR. HAP.   That was rather curious, wasn't it ?

Mrs. Hap. What was ? (*She goes to her chair R. of the table.*)

Mr. Hap. The figure she mentioned—four hundred and twenty pounds.

Mrs. Hap (*standing by her chair*). Oh, no. It was just a figure that came into her head. But I'm glad it's Pie-Face—

(Mr. Hapgood *turns to the fire. Enter* Ted *from the front door. He is looking very pale.*)

Mrs. Hap (*glancing at him*). Ted, are you feeling all right ?

Ted. Yes . . . I'm all right . . .

Mrs. Hap (*concerned*). But you're not. You look awful

Ted. I'm all right, I tell you . . . But there's something—

Mr. Hap (*coming forward*). Don't say *you* are going to be married !

Ted. Yes—I am.

Mr. Hap. Oh, my God ! (*He turns back to the fire.*)

Ted (*moving to the chair above the table; to* Mrs. Hapgood). You think it's rather funny that I should have a girl friend, don't you ? You think I'm too young to fall in love—that Dandy is a silly name for a girl, and that it's a waste of time for you even to ask her here. All right, then—now you've asked for it—because I'm going to marry her right away—

Mrs. Hap (*anxiously*). Ted dear, I think you ought to go to bed.

Ted. I said I felt perfectly well. (*He sits above the table.*)

Mrs. Hap (*gently*). I know you're not—because it's obvious you couldn't marry anybody on your present salary—

Mr. Hap (*sharply*). What's the matter, Ted ?

Ted (*on the verge of breaking down*). Dad . . . it's awful . . . awful . . . We've *got* to be married . . . Dandy is going to have a baby . . .

He covers his face with his hands. They look at him in horror as—

The Curtain *falls.*

SCENE 2.

Scene—*The Same. Two evenings later.*

Mr. Hapgood *is sitting above the table finishing his tea which is laid on a tray. The door is open.* Myra *enters.*

Myra (*coming C.*). Arthur's coming, Dad.

Mr. Hap. Oh, good. Did you find Ted ?

Myra. No. I think he must be out.

Mr. Hap. Oh, well, he'll just have to be surprised.

Myra. Are you nervous ?

Mr. Hap. Are you ?

Myra. I don't mind telling you I'm petrified. So are you.

(*Enter* Arthur. *He is now moustached, self-confident, happy.*)

Mr. Hap. Good. Close the door, Arthur.

(Arthur *closes the door.*)

Give me a cigarette.

Arthur. We'd better all have a drink as well—(*He hands his cigarette case to* Mr. Hapgood *and crosses to the sideboard.*)

Mr. Hap. No, better not. It's unusual at this time of the evening— it might make her wonder . . . Now, listen, both of you. We've got to let this meeting be carried through naturally. No artificial talk or silly remarks. Mother is going to have an awful shock, but she must work out her own salvation.

Arthur (*moving to R. of* Mr. Hapgood). John will see there are no awkward moments.

Myra (*moving to L. of* Mr. Hapgood). So will Phyl.

Mr. Hap. It's an awful pity we couldn't arrange a normal meeting. I'm not sure it wouldn't have been best after all.

Myra. No, I don't agree. If mother knew that they were coming this evening she'd have prepared a hoity-toity speech which would have ruined everything.

Arthur (*the big traveller*). It'd be a darn good thing if we Europeans arranged our marriages on a purely barter basis, like the natives ; then there wouldn't be any of these fearful complications. On the Coast you simply pick out your better half, hand over a fiver and one cow to her family—and that ends all argument.

Myra. How too, too ju-ju !

Arthur (*eyeing* Myra). In some cases, of course, they'll take just the cow . . .

Mr. Hap. Now can either of you think of any hitch that we can be prepared for in advance ? There are no visitors coming, for instance ?

Myra. Not that *I* know of.

Arthur. Nor me.

Mr. Hap. By the way, Myra, George rang me up this afternoon and asked whether he could have a talk with me tonight—

MYRA (*troubled*). Oh, lord . . . Did he say what it was about ?

MR. HAP. No, but he seemed very pleased with himself. Have you any idea what he wants ?

MYRA (*slowly*). No, I haven't.

MR. HAP. I didn't tell him Phyl and John were coming, but I did say tomorrow would be more convenient—(*Listening.*) S'sh—your mother !

(MYRA *crosses to the settee.* MRS. HAPGOOD *enters.*)

MRS. HAP (*coming to L. of* MR. HAPGOOD, *about to pick up the tea tray*). Have you finished dear ?

MR. HAP. Yes, thank you. It was very nice. What was it ?

(MRS. HAPGOOD *gives him an indignant look, picks up the tray and goes to the door with it.*)

MRS. HAP (*turning at the door*). Are you going out tonight, Arthur ?

ARTHUR (*casually*). No, I don't think I shall.

MRS. HAP. Are you, Myra ?

MYRA. No.

MRS. HAP. Nor are you, Billy—so that's all right.

MR. HAP (*sharply*). What is all this about ?

MRS. HAP (*briskly*). We have a visitor coming.

MR. HAP \
ARTHUR } (*together*). { What !
MYRA / { Oh, my God ! / Who on earth— !

MRS. HAP (*surprised*). Is it so odd for us to have a visitor ? What's the matter with you all ?

MR. HAP (*hastily*). Nothing. . . . Just rather a bombshell—the way you came out with it—that's all. Who is it ?

MRS. HAP. Dandy.

MR. HAP. Er—who on earth is Dandy ?

MYRA. My future sister-in-law, of course.

MRS. HAP. Ted asked if I'd let him bring her round. He's so upset. He wants us so much to like her.

MR. HAP. I'm glad you told her to come . . . !

MRS. HAP. We must make the best of it. I won't make the same mistake this time. . . . Tidy up the room a bit, Myra.

(*She goes out.*)

MR. HAP (*hurriedly*). Arthur—quick.

(*He rises and moves to C. ARTHUR follows him.*)

Nip round to the telephone kiosk on the corner and ring them up.
Tell Phyllis what's happened and ask her to put the visit off till
tomorrow.

(ARTHUR *moves up to the door.*)

No, wait—George is coming tomorrow.

MYRA. Don't bother. I can put him off to the day after.

ARTHUR. This is getting complicated. . . . Anyway, Phyl and
John are probably on their way.

MR. HAP. Probably, but it's worth trying. (*As he moves up L. of
ARTHUR.*) Oh, and Arthur—if you can't get them press button B
and get your money back. . . .

(ARTHUR *goes out by the front door.*)

(*He comes down C.*) Never be a father, Myra . . . Thank God
I'm not a rabbit !

MYRA (*moving below the settee and sitting on the R. arm*). Mother is going
to like Dandy eventually.

MR. HAP. What is she like ?

MYRA. What does " amenable " mean ?—because that's what she is.
She sort of does what she's told—

MR. HAP (*smiling*). Oh, does she ?

MYRA. What are you laughing at ?

MR. HAP. Oh, nothing . . . Fancy Ted being a father !

MYRA. And you a grandfather ! Ever thought of that ?

MR. HAP. And you an aunt ! Ever thought of *that* !

MYRA (*shocked*). Eh !

MR. HAP (*gloomily*). Awful, isn't it ? . . . . I'm going into the
garden. Tell Arthur, will you ?

MYRA. All right, Dad.

(*Exit* MR. HAPGOOD. *Left alone,* MYRA *goes to the bookcase and idly
picks up a book, dropping it again with a sigh. She is depressed and
pre-occupied. The window is pushed open and* GEORGE'S *head appears.*)

GEORGE (*exuberantly*). What-ho !

MYRA (*startled*). Pie-Face—

GEORGE. Let me in.

MYRA. But we've got visitors coming—

GEORGE. I can't help that. Anyway, I shan't keep you two minutes. The directors are going to play ! (*Withdrawing his head.*) You let me in . . .

(MYRA *hesitates, then goes out and lets him in at the front door. They enter* GEORGE *is talking eagerly.*)

The Directors are going to play. (*He embraces her.*) . . . Old Henshawe worked it for us. He said they stood out for half an hour on principle. Imagine it—the whole ruddy Board of Directors arguing about—us ! We sail on June the twentieth. I know Mr. Hapgood doesn't want to see me tonight but I had to come round and tell you. I'm glad you're alone ! Give me a kiss.

(MYRA *gives him a lifeless kiss. He looks at her, dismayed.*)

What's the matter ?

MYRA (*bracing herself with an effort*). There's a shock coming . . . You'll have to go without me . . .

(*A pause.*)

GEORGE (*licking his lips*). Well, go on—

MYRA. Ted's made a fool of himself. He and Dandy have got to be married. (*She moves below the settee.*)

GEORGE. Good lord . . . (*He comes to the R. end of the settee.*) But how does that stop you coming with me ?

MYRA (*sitting on the settee*). Georgie, I know this is a jolt for you and I'm . . . so sorry . . . But please try and understand what I'm going to say. I'm not quite clear about it myself—but I know it's right. I'm worried about mother . . .

GEORGE. Did you tell her about the job ?

MYRA. No, there wasn't any point until your directors had made up their minds. She might have had a shock for nothing.

GEORGE (*sitting beside her*). What has she got to be so frightened about ?

MYRA (*taking his hands*). That's what I want you to try and understand. You'll find it a bit of a job, I expect, because your mother is so jolly *normal.* I suppose some people would call mother possessive. Perhaps she is. But I've lived at home with her ever since I left school and I've learnt rather a lot about her. You have to realise that only one thing in the whole world matters to her—Us— the Hapgoods. She never talks of anything or anybody else. And she's no different from any other person who is an expert in a certain line—that's what she is, you know. As a mother she's an absolute genius, and all geniuses are a bit—abnormal. Do you see what I mean ?

GEORGE.   No.

MYRA.   I'm putting it badly.   But the point is this—she wants to go on being the mother of the four Hapgood children.   She overdoes it, of course.   But what lies at the bottom of it ?   Why, the unfortunate fact that she loves us—desperately.   So what on earth can you do ?

GEORGE.   But if she's wrong somebody ought to tell her.

MYRA.   I can't turn round and say, " I know you're terribly fond of me ; I know I'm your last link with all that you've lived for for the past thirty odd years—but nuts to that, I'm off ! "   For one thing I happen to love her, too . . .

GEORGE.   Arthur and Phyl went.   Were they wrong ?

MYRA.   But I'm the last one, Pie-Face, and she's going to need me so badly.   Ted's little affair has knocked her sideways ; I can't leave her at a time like this.

GEORGE.   She would have your father—

MYRA.   He's at business all day.   Think of being alone in a house full of ghosts. . . .   What she'll want is somebody to yank her out of her bedroom every time she slinks up to mope over the family album.   (*She rises and crosses to C.*)

GEORGE (*desperately*).   What about Arthur ?   He'll be at home for the next eighteen weeks—

MYRA.   Arthur !   (*She moves in to the R. arm of the settee.*)   Can you see him mucking about at home always ?   (*Sadly.*)   No Pie-Face, I'm the only one who can help her.   I'm . . . so *sorry* for her . . .

GEORGE.   Myra—what about me . . . . ?

MYRA (*sitting on the arm of the settee*).   Pie-Face, in a strange way I've come to love you even more since I decided not to come with you . . . .   Do you think it was easy for me to tell you ?   (*She rises and moves above the settee.*)

(*Enter* ARTHUR.)

ARTHUR.   Hallo, George !   (*He comes down C.*)

GEORGE (*flatly*).   Hallo, Arthur.   (*He rises*).   Spot of leave ?

ARTHUR.   That's it.   You haven't changed much ?

GEORGE.   Nor have you.   Bit more hairy, perhaps.

ARTHUR (*laughing and stroking his moustache*).   Where's Dad ?

MYRA.   In the garden.   He's been looking for you.

ARTHUR.   Right-o, I'll find him.   See you later, George.

(*He goes out.*)

GEORGE.   Myra, how long must I wait ?

MYRA (*painfully*). Probably until you come home again.

GEORGE. Three years ?

(MYRA *nods*.)

(*He crosses below the table*.) I can see what's going to happen Your mother will get so used to your being at home, and you'll get so used to it yourself that—

MYRA (*sharply*). Pie-Face ! (*She runs to him*.)

GEORGE (*humbly*). I love you so much, Myra . . . .

MYRA (*whispering*). Please don't make it difficult for me ; . . . .

GEORGE (*with a deep sigh*). All right. I'll wait.

MYRA (*almost overcome*). Thank you, darling. (*She kisses him*.)

GEORGE (*holding her*). What would you say if I refused the job and stayed at home near you ?

MYRA (*strongly*). I'd have nothing more to do with you. You've got to take it ; it's a marvellous opportunity.

GEORGE (*pleading*). It's going to be hell, Myra. I'd far sooner stay in England near you.

MYRA (*severely*). Listen to me, George Harris—I'm not marrying anybody without guts . . . . Perhaps you'd better go now, Georgie. (*She leads him towards the door*.) We've got a month together. . . .

(*Enter* ARTHUR *and* MR. HAPGOOD. MYRA *breaks to L. of the table*. GEORGE *continues to the door*.)

MR. HAP. Oh, er, you wanted to have a talk with me, didn't you, George ?

GEORGE. Well, it was nothing very important. . . . Myra can tell you all the news.

MR. HAP. All right, George, good-bye

ARTHUR. See you again, Pie-Face.

GEORGE. Cheerio. (*He goes out*.)

(ARTHUR *crosses above the settee and comes down L*.)

MR. HAP. What was his news ? Anything important ?

MYRA. Well, it was rather. His firm have given him a grand job in Cape Town. He's going in a month's time.

MR. HAP. What does that mean ?

MYRA. I'm afraid it means we can't get married until he gets back in three years time. . . .

MR. HAP. Oh, that's too bad.

MYRA. It's a rule the firm has. He argued with his directors about it, but they refused to play. . . .

MR. HAP. Never mind, you're both very young, dear. It will soon pass.

(*Enter* MRS. HAPGOOD.)

MRS. HAP. I thought I heard George's voice while I was upstairs. Has he gone ? (*She crosses above the table and comes down R. to the work box.*)

MYRA. Yes, just.

(MR. HAPGOOD *crosses to the fire.* ARTHUR *sits on the settee.*)

MRS. HAP (*taking her work basket to the table*). Good. Myra—did you explain why it was . . . . inconvenient to have him here this evening ? (*She sits above the table.*)

MYRA. Yes. Does it matter ?

MRS. HAP (*sitting and commencing work on a pair of socks*). He'll have to know eventually, I suppose. But yes, naturally it matters. I don't like to think of outside people knowing of Ted's disgrace . . . talking about it . . . . (*With spirit.*) If they talk they'll have me to deal with.

ARTHUR. That goes for all of us.

MRS. HAP. Not that I've finished with Ted myself yet—

MYRA (*moving above the table*). Oh, have a heart, mother. He must have gone through hell lately. He's only a kid. (*She turns to the window.*) And so's Dandy. A couple of innocents, that's all they are. (*She sees* PHYLLIS *and* JOHN *through the window.*)

(MRS. HAPGOOD *is seated at the table with her back to the door.* ARTHUR *and* MR. HAPGOOD *stand by the fireplace* MYRA *turns from the window and signs to* MR. HAPGOOD *that* PHYLLIS *and* JOHN *are just coming. She slips out into the hall and lets them in quietly. She returns, crosses above the settee and comes down to the fire.*)

MRS. HAP. It's very sweet of you to stick up for them, Myra, but you can't tell me they didn't know what they were doing. Oh my goodness ! Look at all these holes. I don't know how you boys manage it ! I'll be sorry for your wives, if you ever have any. Were you hard on your clothes when you were a boy, Billy ? . . . . Billy ?

(PHYLLIS *enters, followed by* JOHN. *Affluence has given* PHYLLIS *no exaggerated ideas about dress and simplicity is still her keynote. She comes down and stands above and L. of* MRS. HAPGOOD. JOHN *remains by the door. Still getting no answer,* MRS. HAPGOOD *looks up to find that* MR. HAPGOOD *is staring at somebody behind her.* MRS. HAPGOOD *turns.*)

Phyl . . . .

PHYL (*nervously*).   Hallo, mother . . . .

MRS. HAP.   Oh, Phyl . . . .   (*She rises, takes* PHYLLIS *in her arms and holds her closely, breaking down and weeping.*)

(JOHN *closes the door.*)

PHYL.   Darling, I thought you'd like me to come now—

MRS. HAP.   It was kind of you to come . . . .

PHYL.   I needed you, mother—

MRS. HAP.   Yes, dear . . . .   Yes.   And that is all you need say. That is *all* you need say . . . .   (*She stands away, holding* PHYLLIS *at arms length, looking at her raptly.*)

PHYL (*gently*).   Mother—John . . . .

MRS. HAP (*nervously*).   Your husband . . . .

(JOHN *comes down L. of* PHYLLIS.   MRS. HAPGOOD *takes his hand.*)

JOHN.   Don't you think Phyl is looking well ?

MRS. HAP.   Yes.

JOHN.   Do you think she looks any older ?

MRS. HAP.   Yes—a little—not too much . . . .

JOHN.   Do me a favour, will you, Mrs. Hapgood ?

MRS. HAP.   What is it ?

JOHN.   Ask her if she has been really and truly happy ?

MRS. HAP (*looking at* PHYL).   Have you ?

PHYL.   Yes, mother, really and truly happier than I'd ever dreamed I could be . . . except—

MRS. HAP.   Except ?

PHYL.   That you didn't answer my letters—

(*Over by the fireplace a party has broken out.* MYRA, ARTHUR *and* MR. HAPGOOD *are dancing in a circle, hand in hand.*)

MRS. HAP.   Look at those three fatheads !   (*She turns away to the sideboard where she adjusts the flowers and recovers herself.*)

(*There is a burst of laughter.* MYRA *rushes to* PHYLLIS.)

MYRA.   Phyl, my old hen-sparrow !   Gosh, you look good !   (*She flings her arms round her.*)

PHYL.   How is the old war-horse ?

MYRA.   Fine !

ARTHUR (*moving below the settee to C.*).   Welcome back to the moated grange, Phyl !

PHYL (*crossing to* ARTHUR).   Hallo, Arthur !   Oh, look, mother—the
moustache !

JOHN (*moving to* MYRA).   Hallo !

MYRA.   Hallo !   I kiss you, don't I ?

JOHN.   It's practically a duty.   (*He kisses her.*)

(ARTHUR *moves to* JOHN.   *Myra crosses to* MRS. HAPGOOD *and puts
an arm round her.*)

ARTHUR.   Hallo, John !   It's good to see you again.

JOHN.   Thanks, old boy.   You're looking fit.   Good tour ?

ARTHUR.   Magnificent.

(PHYLLIS *crosses to* MRS. HAPGOOD, *and they hold hands, smiling at one
another but saying nothing.*)

What about a drink ?   Have we got anything, mother ?

MRS. HAP.   There's a bottle in the sideboard.

ARTHUR.   What is it ?

MRS. HAP.   I don't know.   I got it at Mr. Jones'.   It says " Port
Style " on the label.

(ARTHUR *takes the bottle from the upstage cupboard of the sideboard.*   MYRA
*takes eight port glasses from the downstage cupboard.   They fill the
glasses together.*)

(MRS. HAPGOOD *sits* R. *of the table.*)

PHYL (*looking round the room with shining eyes*).   Oh, it's good to be back
. . . . . Everything the same . . . . (*She crosses to* MR. HAPGOOD.)
Still got your old clock, Daddy !   Still striking five at eight and
fourteen at one ?

MR. HAP.   Something like that.   It's good to have you back—isn't
it, Mary ?

MRS. HAP.   Yes, dear . . . .   (*To* PHYLLIS.)   We'll go   upstairs
together soon and have a long, long chat.

PHYL.   I'd like that more than anything.   (*She sits on the settee.*)

JOHN (*coming behind the settee, slightly* L. *of* PHYLLIS).   Am I to be left
out in the cold ?

(MYRA *crosses with two glasses, gives one to* PHYLLIS *and one to* MR.
HAPGOOD *and crosses back to the sideboard.*)

We'll have a long chat, eh, Mr. Hapgood ?   For a start you can
explain, as an old hand at this parenthood business, why *I* should
be feeling so physically uncomfortable ?

(ARTHUR *takes a glass himself and gives one to* MRS. HAPGOOD.   *He stands down stage of her against the sideboard.* Myra *crosses with two more glasses, one of which she gives to* John, *the other she keeps herself and stands by the chair above the table.*)

Mr. Hap (*smiling*). They say it's quite natural, John—but I must say it sounds a bit premature in your case.

John. My own theory is we're going to have twins. Phyl will have one and I shall have the other.

(*All now have drinks.*)

Myra. What's the toast ?

Mr. Hap. Well, here's to—

(*The slamming of the front door interrupts him.*)

Mrs. Hap. Oh, Billy, I'd forgotten—!

(*The door is thrown open and* Ted *appears with* Dandy Westmore. *He has a protecting arm round her waist.* Dandy *is an insipidly pretty girl of the same age as* Ted. *She is petrified with fright and when she speaks is practically inaudible.*)

Ted (*defiantly*). Mother, this is Dandy.

Mrs. Hap. How do you do, Dandy ? I'm so glad Ted brought you.

Dandy. Th-thank you, Mrs. Hapgood . . . .

Ted. Dad, this is—(*Catching sight of* Phyllis.) Hallo, Phyl !

Phyl. Hallo, Ted ! You and Dandy are just in time for a drink.

(Arthur *fills two more glasses.*)

Myra. Two more drinks, Arthur ! (*To* Dandy.) Dad was just going to make a speech. You've saved us !

Mr. Hap (*nervously moving C. and approaching* Dandy). How do you do, Dandy ? (*He strains to catch her reply, but only her lips move. He shakes hands with her.*) Er—have you got any other name ?

Dandy (*audible in parts*). My proper name is Genevieve. It's only Ted calls me Dandy.

Mr. Hap. I expect we shall call you Dandy as well. Will that be all right ?

Dandy. Yes . . . . thank you . . . .

Arthur. Two drinks coming up, Ted—

(Ted *and* Dandy *move up C.* Arthur *crosses to them with two glasses.* Ted *remains steadfastly at her side looking round suspiciously, ready to deal with anything savouring of a slight on his lady.*)

(*To* Dandy.) I'm Arthur, in case Ted forgets.

DANDY (*mouthing*). How do you do ? (*They shake hands.*)

MYRA (*leading* JOHN *forward*). That's John Neilson. You'll find he smells wonderful—

(ARTHUR *crosses to* R.)

TED (*curtly*). She's being funny.

JOHN (*bowing*). My aroma is at your disposal !

(*There is a roar of laughter.* DANDY *looks round with a startled smile.*)

TED (*snarling*). What's so damn' funny ?

MR. HAP (*hastily*). That's all right, Ted—nothing to get upset about.

TED (*tensely*). But you must have laughed at something. I didn't bring Dandy here so that everybody could make a joke of her— (*He is about to lead her out.*)

MR. HAP. Ted, don't look for trouble where it doesn't exist. We laughed because John was offering Dandy his aroma—that's all.

(TED *subsides, muttering.*)

Now, what about this toast ? Here's to us all, eh ? (*Raising his glass.*)   Mary my love . . . . Phyl. . . . John . . . . Dandy . . . . all of us

MRS. HAP. Not forgetting old George !

PHYL. Of course ! Pie-Face ! George *Job* Harris !

ARTHUR. Good old Stonewall Jackson ! Speech, Myra !

MYRA (*suddenly subdued*). I can't make speeches—

(*There is a chorus of protests.*)

It's so silly to make a speech about Pie-Face . . . . You all know him . . . . You know he's all right . . . . I said I couldn't make a speech—

MR. HAP (*gently*). Let's simply say, " Good old Pie-Face "—and leave it at that, shall we ? I don't think Myra is in the mood for speeches tonight—

MRS. HAP (*concerned*). Myra, what has happened, dear ? There's nothing wrong ?

MR. HAP (*to* MYRA). We'd better tell them, Myra . . . . . (*To the others.*) They're still going to be married, of course, but—well, there's been a bit of a disappointment, that's all. Pie-Face has got to go abroad for his firm. They can't get married for three years—that's when he gets back.

ARTHUR   } (*together*). { Where's he off to ?
MRS. HAP.   }   { But how disappointing . . . .

MR. HAP. It's bad luck, isn't it ?

Myra.   I'll tell you all about it later.   Let's talk about something more cheerful, shall we ?

Mr. Hap.   His directors are not very helpful.   They've refused to waive the rule about wives—

Myra.   Oh, Dad, some other time, please.

Mr. Hap.   All right, Myra.   Now let's drink this toast.   Here's to us all . . . .   Mary, my love . . . .   John . . . .   Phyl. . . . .

(*They toast each other and drink.*)

John.   I could reply if called upon—

Mr. Hap.   Let's hear your reply !

Phyl.   Make it short, darling !

(John *comes down C.*)

John.   My dear father-in-law, my dear mother-in-law (*he puts out his hand to* Phyllis.   *She rises and stands by him.*)   All I want to say is thank you—for Phyllis . . . .   (*To* Mr. Hapgood.)   Mr. Hapgood, I should like to see your garden.   I hear you are shockingly conceited about your roses—

(Phyllis *sits on the settee.*   Ted *finishes his glass and puts it ana* Dandy's *on the table.*)

Mr. Hap.   Oh, I see.   Well, of course . . . .   (*Modestly.*)   As a matter of fact they were much better last year.

John.   They always are !   (*He goes up C.*)   Dandy, have you seen the garden ?   As co-in-laws-to-be we must get together and discuss our newly acquired relatives.   (*He offers her his arm.*)

Ted.   Wait a minute, Neilson.   I think I'd better come as well . . . .

John.   Very well—although I promise she'll come to no harm.

(*He takes* Dandy's *arm and leads her to the door.   They go out.*)

Phyl.   Ted, there's no need for you to go really.

Ted.   Well, she's a bit shy—

(Myra *puts empty glasses on the sideboard.*)

Phyl.   Nobody is ever shy with John—

Mrs. Hap (*suddenly ; moving up C.*).   Ted—close the door—quickly. Look Billy—do you notice anything ?   We're all together—just the six of us !

Arthur.   Good Lord, so we are !

(*The children look at each other, startled and a little embarrassed.*   Mrs. Hapgood *puts her arms round* Ted's *and* Arthur's *waists.*)

MRS. HAP. Arthur . . . . Phyl . . . . Ted . . . . Myra . . . .

MYRA (*severely*). Mother—careful. You know you'll burst into tears in a minute.

MRS. HAP. I don't care. I'm the only one in this family who isn't ashamed of tears. Billy, aren't you proud of them ?

MR. HAP. They could have been spanked a bit more, perhaps—

TED. That refers to me, I suppose ?

MRS. HAP (*spiritedly*). Yes, Ted—that *does* refer to you. You always were headstrong and heedless, and you deserve all the trouble and worry you've had. (*She comes down C. below the table.*) What I can't believe, Billy, is that I used to bath them all in front of that fire when they were babies !

MR. HAP. In a little round tub ! And me busy with the power puff !

(MRS. HAPGOOD *crosses down* R.)

ARTHUR. Oh, my God !

MRS. HAP. How I should have laughed at the time if I'd thought Arthur would one day have a moustache !

MR. HAP. You'd have laughed even more if he'd had one then.

ARTHUR. Look—let's change the subject—

MYRA. No, we won't. It's the best joke we've had for years. I think it's the scraggiest, mangiest bit of face-fungus . . . .

(ARTHUR *goes to seize* MYRA *and there is a scuffle. He chases her down stage between the table and the sideboard, across to the fireplace, up* L. *of the settee.*)

PHYLLIS. Leave her alone, you great oaf . . . .

ARTHUR. You keep out of this . . . . (*He grabs a cushion.*)

(MYRA *runs behind the settee to* C.)

TED (*joining the fray on* ARTHUR's *side*). Whoopee ! (*He seizes* MYRA.)

(ARTHUR *turns and goes up* C. *He is* R., TED *is* L., *with* MYRA *between them.* ARTHUR *raises the cushion over* MYRA's *head.* PHYLLIS *jumps up and moves behind* TED *pulling him down, and falling with him.*)

MRS. HAPGOOD. Phyl, be very careful, dear. (*She watches them, her eyes sparkling with happiness.*)

(ARTHUR *goes to the assistance of* PHYLLIS. *He throws the cushion on to the settee. He and* TED *help* PHYLLIS *up.* MYRA *crosses to* R.)

MR. HAP. That will do, now. Arthur—Phyl—stop it.

(PHYLLIS, ARTHUR *and* TED *separate, laughing.*)

PHYL. I'm wrecked ! (*Glancing down at her leg.*) Damn, look at that stocking—it's started a ladder. (*She moves to the chair L. of the table and puts her foot on it.*)

MRS HAP (*rising*). Stand still, dear. I'll catch it with a needle and thread before it runs. (*She moves down R. to the work box.*)

TED. I think I'd better go and find Dandy—

MYRA. For heaven's sake, boy, take a rest ! She's all right.

(TED *goes out.*)

ARTHUR. Let's all go in the garden. I'll put some deck chairs out. Come on, Myra, give me a hand.

MYRA. All right. (*To the others.*) Are you coming ?

PHYL } (*together*). { I'll come when this is finished. (*She sits on the table.*)
MR. HAP } { Yes, we'll follow you later.

(ARTHUR *and* MYRA *go out.*)

MRS. HAP. All the cotton here is the wrong colour. I've got just the right one up in the bedroom, if only I can lay my hand on it. Keep still, dear—

(*She goes out.*)

PHYL (*at once, in excitement*). Daddy, it's a lot of rot about Myra and Pie-face

MR. HAP (*moving towards C. ; startled*). What is a lot of rot ?

PHYL. They could marry tomorrow if only Myra wasn't such an idiot—

MR. HAP. What do you mean ?

PHYL. We met Pie-Face at the gate. He looked as though he'd just had a whipping. We had to ask him what was wrong. At first he wouldn't say, then he swore us to secrecy and out it all came. His directors did agree. It was she who said " No."

MR. HAP. Why ?

PHYL. Because she's the last of us to be left at home and she thinks it would be unfair to leave mother alone. Oh, Daddy, it's such a shame. She's such a good scout—and Pie-Face, too ; he's such a sweet old fathead. They *must* get married. (*Appalled.*) Think of it—three years !

MR. HAP (*heavily*). I thought there was something funny. Yes, three years is too long . . . . much too long.

(MRS. HAPGOOD *enters.* MR. HAPGOOD *sits on the settee.*)

MRS. HAP (*coming to* PHYLLIS). Here it is—the exact colour—(*She begins the repair to* PHYLLIS's *stocking*.) Aren't you going into the garden with the others, Billy ?

MR. HAP. No, I'll wait for you.

MRS. HAP. So you're happy, Phyl ?

PHYL. Yes.

MRS. HAP. I'm sure you are . . . . very happy . . . .

PHYL. It's such fun looking after him ! Do you know, mother, it's surprising how helpless he is in quite a number of ways. (*Laughing*) I often wonder what he did without me ! You'd think he'd be very sophisticated and self-confident about every little problem that faced him. But it was I who took the dog to the vet to be put to sleep. As a matter of fact it was I who decided that we should have this baby. John was afraid it was going to be too much for me !

MRS. HAP. Well, of course, men are very impractical . . . . There you are, dear, that should hold until you reach home. (*She moves above the table to her work basket and takes out some letters.*)

PHYL. Thank you, Mummy. (*She moves to the door.*) Are you coming Daddy ?

MR. HAP. You go ahead, Phyl. We'll follow in a few minutes.

PHYL. Right you are.

MRS. HAP. Phyl—(*She moves towards her.*)

PHYL. Yes, mother ? (*She turns and meets* MRS. HAPGOOD *at R.C.*)

MRS. HAP (*handing* PHYLLIS *a packet of letters*). You were never forgotten Phyl !

PHYL (*kissing her*). Darling mother.

MRS. HAP. Now I can burn them. (*She takes the letters back.*)

(PHYLLIS *goes to the door.*)

MR. HAP. Oh, Phyl—it'll be all right . . . . Don't worry . . . .

PHYL. Thank you, Pops !

(*She goes out.*)

MRS. HAP (*moving R. above the table.*) Not worry ? What about ? (*She goes down R. to the work box.*)

MR. HAP. Mary, I wasn't telling you the truth just now about George and Myra. His firm have agreed to let him take her with him to Cape Town—

MRS. HAP (*faltering*). Did she tell you herself . . . ?

MR.. HAP. No. She didn't want us to know.

MRS. HAP. But why ? (*She moves up R.*)

Mr. Hap. She was afraid of how you would take it. She doesn't want to hurt you any more.

Mrs. Hap. Are you sure of that ? (*She crosses above the table.*)

Mr. Hap. Yes. George told Phyllis and Phyllis told me . . . . Well, Mary ?

Mrs. Hap (*coming to the chair L. of the table ; wretchedly*). Can't we talk this over tomorrow—It's been such a difficult day—with Phyllis and John and everything—

Mr. Hap. I'd rather settle it tonight.

Mrs. Hap. What is the hurry ?

Mr. Hap. George is waiting in the garden. His firm want the answer tomorrow. We don't want him to have a sleepless night, do we?

Mrs. Hap. If—if Myra goes we'll be alone . . . .

Mr. Hap. Mary, do you love me still ?

Mrs. Hap (*surprised*). Of course I do. (*She crosses to him.*) I've always loved you. (*She sits on the settee, R. of him.*)

Mr. Hap. And I you. I always shall. (*He takes her hand.*) After we were married we had two wonderful years together—just the two of us. . . . Then the children started coming, and somehow things became a little different. Naturally you couldn't give me quite so much of your time, and I was busy trying to provide for you all. Well, we've been very happy together. They're fine kids and I'm as proud of them as you are. But now—well— there's nothing more we can do for them and—this may sound funny, perhaps, but—I rather want them to leave us to ourselves. You know, they don't need us any more—they've been trying to tell us that. You refused to listen . . . .

Mrs. Hap. Billy !

Mr. Hap. I'm sorry, but I've got to say this.

Mrs. Hap. What did I do that was wrong ? Haven't I loved them enough ? You think I've failed as a mother ?

Mr. Hap. No, Mary, no—

Mrs. Hap. I don't think I have. Their happiness has always been my happiness. I've made mistakes, perhaps—yes. I know I was wrong about Arthur and Phyl, because they've so obviously found happiness in their own way—

Mr. Hap. As a man and a woman.

Mrs. Hap. Yes. . . . Perhaps that was my biggest mistake ; I'd seen them only as children. Billy, it's so hard for a mother to realise that her children are no longer children.

Mr. Hap. But we shall always be their mother and father, Mary. They'll always come back to us.

Mrs. Hap (*with a little shiver*).   But the house will seem so lonely . . .

Mr. Hap (*unhappily*).   There's nothing I can say to that. . . .   I'd do my best to make you happy—

Mrs. Hap.   Oh, my dear, I didn't mean to hurt you.   Of course Myra must go.   After all I shall have one child to look after—

Mr. Hap.   One child ?

Mrs. Hap.   My Billykins !

Mr. Hap (*startled*).   " Billykins " ?   I thought you'd forgotten—

Mrs. Hap.   I haven't forgotten anything.   In those days *you* had a moustache, and you used to part your hair in the middle.   And you fancied yourself in pointed brown shoes—and a straw hat—and a cane—

Mr. Hap.   Do you remember all that ?

Mrs. Hap.   Of course I do . . . .   Oh, how strange to have the house to ourselves ; to have only ourselves to think about . . . .   We might go and live in the country—

Mr. Hap.   Why not ?

Mrs. Hap.   Dorking !   Of course—Dorking !.

Mr. Hap (*happily*).   Dorking—yes !   The number of times we've passed through it and said, " What a nice place to live in ! "

Mrs. Hap.   We could take some of this furniture.   If we have a smaller house we wouldn't need it all.

Mr. Hap.   Yes, we could take that, and—(*he points at particular pieces of furniture.*)   We won't take that damn' clock !   It's never understood kind treatment !

Mrs. Hap.   Poor old clock . . . .

Mr. Hap (*rising and moving C.*).   And now, my love, shall we go and tell Myra ?

Mrs. Hap (*rising, drawing a deep breath*).   Yes . . . . all right . . .

Mr. Hap (*linking his arm through hers*).   We'll try and find a small house near Box Hill.   And I want a dog—I've always wanted a dog.

(*He breaks off as the clock begins to chime and stops to listen.   The chimes mount steadily and serenely to eight—and then stop.   Mr. Hapgood looks at the clock, astonished.*)

What's the time, dear ?

Mrs. Hap.   Eight o'clock.   (*She looks at her wrist watch.*)

Mr. Hap.   Well !   Its *struck* right !   (*He crosses to the clock and picks it up.*)   We'll take it with us.

He crosses to Mrs. Hapgood *and they go up·C.*   Mrs. Hapgood *on his R. arm.   Before they reach the door—*

The Curtain *Falls.*

FURNITURE AND PROPERTY PLOT.

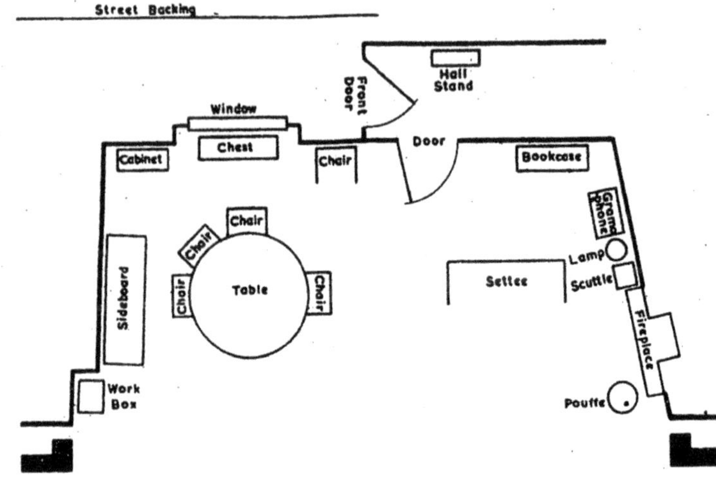

GROUND PLAN.

ACT I.

On Stage—

Dining table.

4 Chairs set as in Ground Plan round table.

Work box. *In it*: work basket, sewing, knitting, socks.

Sideboard. *On it*: runner, silver-framed photograph, 2 tumblers, cruet, silver teapot, bowl of fruit, silver salver, lamp, ash tray.

> *In downstage cupboard*: 8 port glasses.

> *In upstage cupboard*: soda syphon, whisky, port, 2 tumblers, bottle of ale.

> *In drawer*: table cloth, 3 forks, 3 dessert forks, 3 dessert spoons, 2 serving spoons, 3 dinner knives, bottle opener, oil-can, pen-knife.

Cabinet. *In it*: 2 silver cups, ornaments.

Oak chest.

Chair, R. of door.

Bookcase.

Gramophone. *On it*: vase of flowers.

Standard lamp.

Coal scuttle.

Settee. *On it*: 2 loose cushions.

Pouffe.

Fire-irons.

On mantelpiece : clock, 2 silver-framed photographs, 2 silver candlesticks, 2 ash trays, pair of scissors.
In fender : pair of slippers.
In Hall : Hall stand, chair.

Off Stage L.

Exercise book, fountain pen, pencil (MYRA).
Tray with 3 plates, water jug, milk jug, cup, saucer, sugar basin (MRS. HAPGOOD).
Evening paper (MR. HAPGOOD).
2 plates of food (MRS. HAPGOOD).
Plate of food (PHYLLIS).

Personal—

MR. HAPGOOD : pipe, pouch, matches, cigarettes.
ARTHUR : cigarettes.
TED : lighter.
JOHN : cigarette case.

At the end of Act strike : Bread board and knife from sideboard. Apron from settee. Flowers from gramophone. Slippers from fender.

move : Chair from up R. of table, above sideboard. Chair from L. of table, to R. of bookcase. Bowl of flowers from table to bookcase. Whisky and syphon to sideboard cupboard.

ACT II. SCENE 1.

On Stage :

On settee : book, bag of sweets.
On sideboard : work basket, vase of daffodils.

Off Stage L.—Music (GEORGE).

Personal—(GEORGE) cigarettes, matches, wallet.

At end of Scene strike : used tumblers.

SCENE 2.

On Stage—

On table : clock from mantelpiece, oil can, screwdriver, pen-knife.

On settee : magazines.

Off Stage L.—2 prayer books.

At the end of Act strike : Prayer books, flowers, Myra's gloves.
replace : Clock on mantelpiece.
change : Curtains and cushions.

ACT III. SCENE 1.

On Stage—
  On gramophone : vase of roses.
  On sideboard : vase of flowers, bottle of ale, bottle opener.
  On chair R. *of door* : Tennis racket.
  On chest : magazines.
  On pouffe : magazines.

  Set : chair from R. of bookcase in front of fire with 2 sheets over
    back to air ; chair from above sideboard L. of the table.

Off Stage L.—
  Telegram.
  Pipe (MRS. HAPGOOD).

SCENE 2.

On stage :
  Replace : Work basket in work box.   Put 3 letters in basket.
  On table : tea tray, laid for one.

Off Stage L.—Needle and cotton (MRS. HAPGOOD).

www.ingramcontent.com/pod-product-compliance
Ingram Content Group UK Ltd.
Pitfield, Milton Keynes, MK11 3LW, UK
UKHW021823150726
7214IPUK00017B/281